I0450686

Climbing Out Of
Autism One Bite At A Time

◆

Climbing Out Of Autism One Bite At A Time

◆

A Step By Step Manual
For Recovery and Developmental Gain

Michelle Cheney

Writers Club Press
San Jose New York Lincoln Shanghai

Climbing Out Of Autism One Bite At A Time
A Step By Step Manual
For Recovery and Developmental Gain

All Rights Reserved © 2001 by Michelle Cheney

No part of this book may be reproduced or transmitted in any
form or by any means, graphic, electronic, or mechanical,
including photocopying, recording, taping, or by any
information storage retrieval system, without the
permission in writing from the publisher.

Writers Club Press
an imprint of iUniverse.com, Inc.

For information address:
iUniverse.com, Inc.
5220 S 16th, Ste. 200
Lincoln, NE 68512
www.iuniverse.com

The information presented herein is intended to be informative and to
provide insight regarding autism as a progressive, systemic, allergic response
due to dietary and environmental factors. It is not intended to act as, or
substitute for, medical advice, and does not contain treatment
recommendations for the public. Please seek the advice of
a licensed physician or naturopathic doctor before
implementing the suggestions outlined in this text.

ISBN: 0-595-18399-9

Printed in the United States of America

Dedication

I dedicate this work to every person who has stayed awake, night after night, wondering what could be done to help a child climb out of the dark abyss called autism.

Additionally, I dedicate this work to its ultimate benefactor, my beautiful son, Raja, whose very existence has been instrumental in exalting mine from the moment of conception. Because of you, I know how to love. I love you deeply and eternally.

Contents

Acknowledgments

There are many people I wish to publicly thank for the support that made this publication possible.

Thank you to my husband, Larry Umthun, who has stayed up all hours of the night to hear me articulate yet another theory related to autism, who never grows tired or impatient in giving me the time and place to research my ideas. This book would not have been possible without you.

Thank you to Bob Wood, whose constant encouragement has been a lifeline and whose editorial skills improved the quality of craftsmanship and readability.

Thank you to Marina McMillan, whose friendship and emotional support provides sustenance when I grow weary, confused, or overwhelmed, and whose ability to make me laugh or make me think deliver just what I need when I need it.

Thank you to Sindy Rae McCord, an occupational therapist whom I befriended through Raja's first evaluation. It was you who handed me Karyn Seroussi's article on curing her son's autism using dietary intervention. Without you, Raja would not be where he is today. You are a kindred soul. Your holistic approach is a treasure to the special needs community.

Thank you to Barbara Raskob and Joan Aragon, who made time in their busy schedules to read this manuscript and provide feedback during the final phase.

Thank you to many people who have showered Raja and me with kindness, help, and emotional support, including:

My father, Bill Cheney, my grandfather, Andrew Goulart, and my sister, Roxanne Nava, for calling, writing, financial support, and gifts that made the rough times smoother; Vicki Galindo, for listening and caring so deeply; Jen Wood, for constant encouragement and excellent educational gifts; Dr. Ragle and Kathy, for extending yourselves to Raja in a loving, professional capacity; the special needs parents with whom I have shared struggles, knowing both laughter and tears; Monica Dwyer, Jeanne Smith, and Amie Rumbo, for constantly handing me helpful information; and Karyn Seroussi and Lisa Lewis, whom I have never met, but whose pioneering work with dietary intervention for autistic children laid the groundwork for this approach. I am personally indebted to you both for helping me help my son. Thank you.

Introduction

My husband, Larry Umthun, and I are the proud parents of a beautiful, autistic son named Raja, whose inspirational and ongoing recovery provided the impetus to write this book. At nearly three years old, Raja was evaluated as developmentally delayed. Eight months later, he was diagnosed with autism. Since autism effects family dynamics as well as the afflicted individual, my son's continuing recovery has not only helped him, but has dramatically improved our family life as well.

Prior to Raja's diagnosis, we tried several interventions without success. However, we achieved measurable results within two weeks of implementing Comprehensive Organic Intervention. Comprehensive Organic Intervention is a systematic approach designed to facilitate recovery and developmental gain by empowering parents to identify and remove the influences that negatively impact a child mentally, physically, emotionally, socially, and behaviorally.

Although ignorant of his symptoms at the time, Raja had many autistic characteristics at birth. As an infant and young toddler, Raja's symptoms were mainly physical: frequent waking, constipation, colic, undigested food in his stools, inexplicably decaying teeth, assorted skin problems, and unusual sensitivity to strangers, light, heat, and sound. After his first birthday, the manifestations became both physical and cognitive, although the cognitive indicators were subtle and insidious. Raja's eye contact diminished. He was not interested in toys. Although he was around other children, Raja seemed aloof, as though things that interested other children were tedious and boring to him. He was a sloppy eater and preferred not to use utensils. He could not do some of the things his developmental peers could do, like turning a doorknob. Even when he was two years old, I was advised to give him a little time and see if he would come around. Tragically, as time wore on, Raja's undetected autism exacerbated.

Raja was nearing his third birthday when a physical by a new pediatrician yielded a referral to a local program for developmental evaluation based on language delay. After four hours, the team of evaluators classified Raja as developmentally delayed. Once I received a label for Raja's condition, I asked every professional I encountered how a child became developmentally delayed. To my amazement, no one knew. I asked what could be done about Raja's developmental delay. I was told to put him in therapy. I asked how long it would take for him to catch up with his peers using four weekly therapies. I was told they did not know.

Meanwhile, many of Raja's manifestations remained the same while others got worse. His teeth continued decaying. He continued to be constipated. His limited vocabulary disappeared entirely. He ran crying from a hairbrush or toothbrush, screaming constantly while they were applied. He stopped using eating utensils, crayons, and pencils. He continued waking frequently. He continued distancing himself from his toys, his peers, and his desire to make eye contact. He stopped indicating that he was listening. He became terrorized by loud sounds and would run, scream, or cling when startled. He developed a fear of strangers and dislike of unfamiliar places. If he awoke and I was not beside him, he would panic and cry, frantically running to find me. Exhibiting many autistic tendencies, Raja was diagnosed with autism eight months after being classified as developmentally delayed.

Fortunately, because I had suspected Raja was autistic prior to his diagnosis, I began looking for an appropriate intervention. Painfully, I had watched my darling infant son become a reclusive, frightened, antisocial island who desired no human contact but mine. Instead of sleeping, I would lie in bed asking myself over and over what could be causing Raja's disturbing entrance into the dark abyss called autism. I entertained suggestions that Raja might not be speaking because I met all his wants, negating the need to speak. I considered the possibility that he did not want peer-age friends because I spent too much time playing games he enjoyed so he did not desire the company of other children. I questioned the advice that Raja should be forced to endure things he clearly could not tolerate to "toughen him up" because I "babied" him too much. After careful examination, none of these suggestions made sense so I expanded my search by comparing human infant development to other mammalian development.

After hours of logical analysis, I noted that developmental achievement in humans and other mammals appears to be a natural outcome when organic processes are normally functioning. I then speculated that the behaviors resulting in diagnosable autism were actually organic processes gone awry. I felt certain that I could test the efficacy of organic intervention if provided the right road map. After many unsuccessful attempts, a friend handed me an article outlining a diet used by the parent of an autistic boy that had facilitated his eventual recovery. That article marked the beginning of the testing and research leading to Comprehensive Organic Intervention. Nine months after being diagnosed with autism and without the use of additional therapies, Raja is delightful—talking, potty trained, dressing and undressing himself, engaging in imaginary play, displaying empathy, and enjoying the company of other children—thanks to Comprehensive Organic Intervention.

As you may have suspected, Comprehensive Organic Intervention promotes developmental gain through dietary and environmental intervention designed to eliminate the obstacles that retard or prohibit cognitive growth and behavioral stability. If this is the first time you have encountered this concept, you may be surprised that certain foods and non-food substances substantially aggravate autistic characteristics and that recovery is possible simply by avoiding these triggers. While much of the published research regarding the connection between autism and diet comes from England, the research and experimentation herein validates those findings, evident in the physical, mental, emotional, social, and behavioral recovery of my son. Although I cannot predict the level of recovery your child will experience by implementing this approach, I fully believe that complete recovery is possible. Comprehensive Organic Intervention empowers you to promote your child's healing and extend opportunities for him to experience and express his full potential.

Comprehensive Organic Intervention is a two-pronged approach that attempts to discover and eliminate the food and non-food substances that diminish an autistic child's ability to achieve developmental gain verbally, socially, behaviorally, intellectually, and physically. The first step is dietary intervention. Dietary intervention utilizes casein-free, gluten-free guidelines, venturing into relationships between sugar and tactile defensiveness, carbohydrates and joint/muscle pain, and fats and language. The second step is environmental intervention. Environmental intervention attempts to discover and eliminate the non-food substances that inhibit developmental gain through contact. Recovery is facilitated through identification and removal of dietary and environmental triggers that thwart homeostasis, a necessary condition for developmental gain.

It is my firm belief that the behaviors resulting in diagnosable autism are the product of progressive, systemic, allergic responses effecting an individual mentally, physically, emotionally, socially, and behaviorally. As reactions are triggered and compounded in everyday experiences such as eating and bathing, the individual is unable to stabilize before the next meal or activity delivers another onslaught of triggers. The cumulative, systemic effect results in diagnosable autism. Recovery becomes possible by removing the food and non-food substances that trigger reactions. The cause and cumulative effect of reactions will be explored in the Appendix. However, it is not necessary to read or understand the information therein to be successful using this approach. The technical information is presented in relation to the development of this approach and may or may not be of interest to you.

Many authors have contributed knowledge used in developing this approach, including *The Cure For All Diseases* by Dr. Hulda Clark, *Special Diets For Special Kids* by Lisa Lewis, Ph.D., *Eat Right For Your Type* by Peter D'Adamo,N.D., *The Carbohydrate Addict's Diet* by Drs. Rachel and Richard Heller, *Sugar Blues* by William Dufty, and *The Crazy Makers* by Carol Simontachi. Additionally, I have reviewed literature related to allergies written by the National Institute of Health. Finally, Raja has completed more than ten sessions of N.A.E.T treatments for allergy elimination (Nambudripad's Allergy Elimination Technique, named after Dr. Nambudripad who developed the technique). However, the most interesting and relevant information comes from my husband, Larry Umthun, whose ability to feel, articulate, time, and document his reactions to dietary and environmental substances is invaluable. Thus, Comprehensive Organic Intervention combines experience, observation, and research, striving to deliver an approach that is both sound and practical.

The purpose of this book is to build on the information offered in casein-free, gluten-free circles by going one step further in encouraging and empowering you to create for your child the foundation he needs to promote developmental gain. I have attempted to provide a model and to share our experiences as a resource for avoiding the things we believe to be harmful to autistic children. We parents are the real pioneers in autistic research. Our close observation and documentation may someday help the medical and psychological communities solve the mystery of autism. Lofty goals aside, the real intention here is to provide the tools needed to promote developmental gain and normalcy in your child. I have endeavored to be as thorough as possible, hoping that my attention to detail will facilitate your expedited success.

Comprehensive Organic Intervention represents a lifestyle requiring attention, reliability, and a long-term commitment to produce results. This is not a magic bullet nor is it a hit-and-miss approach. It is a foundation that provides a framework for learning and developmental gain to occur. In order to build a solid foundation and framework, it is necessary to vow 100% commitment and strive to uphold this at all times. To this end, you will find recipes, tips for unusual circumstances, and suggestions for holidays and other special occasions to make the transition easier.

We will open by sharing Raja's story and the reasons we chose dietary intervention, discussing the creation of a stable state, casein-free/gluten-free foods, sugars, carbohydrates, fats, and the Food and Reaction Journal. We will then explore environmental factors, including a list of substitutions for safe use. Additionally, we will tackle practical situations, recipes, and suggestions for where to go from here. Finally, the Appendix provides technical information related to allergies and the immune system, including my theory and research regarding autism as a progressive, systemic, allergic response.

If there is one insight that I hope this book successfully conveys, it is that autistic children are in a constant state of physical pain, and that this physical pain is the impetus for their enigmatic social and behavioral manifestations. Diagnosable autism is not merely a brain dysfunction. It is the result of a systemic immune response that creates significant and sustained pain. This simple understanding has given me phenomenal compassion for Raja, as well as tremendous respect for how well he coped on a daily basis while under such physical duress. Additionally, it has fortified my tenacity in rigorously maintaining this approach. Without it, Raja would not only be manifesting symptoms of diagnosable autism, he would be experiencing considerable physical suffering. Comprehensive Organic Intervention is not just an approach to autism recovery; it is an act of love.

In conclusion, writing this book has allowed me several discoveries from hindsight. First, discovering the cause of autism is an urgent goal that may be best facilitated in reverse—by dismantling autism's stranglehold, then testing hypotheses once individuals have entered recovery. Second, accomplishing such a goal requires a team approach, combining talented medical and psychological professionals willing to piece together a puzzle that contains both medical and psychological components. Third, since there is compelling evidence that autistic children are in pain, and since consciously allowing suffering is inhumane, it is time we begin validating anecdotal testimony with scientific testing regarding the relationship between food and the immune response. A creative team of hands-on medical and psychological professionals could easily produce a healing and testing environment that would serve dual purposes. Until then, ending autism's cruel, unnecessary, and prolonged suffering will remain a parent's responsibility. I pray that this book reaches every parent who is willing to work to free his child of autism's heavy chains.

I echo the sentiments of many parents of autistic children when I state that living with my son's autism is the single most grievous and demanding experience I have ever endured; every day with autism is a losing battle. I cannot bear the thought of another parent helplessly watching his child slip away thinking nothing can be done when dietary and environmental changes can facilitate recovery and developmental gain. Thus, I hope these pages provide encouragement, empowerment, and guidelines for facilitating recovery from autism. Finally, while this book was ultimately created to help parents seeking healing for their children, I also hope it is applicable for professional and institutional environments.

May the use of Comprehensive Organic Intervention bring your child and family the hope and continuous healing it has delivered to us.

The Choice for Dietary Intervention

My favorite picture of my son, Raja, is an oversized photograph that graces the wall above our couch with an ear-to-ear grin and an expression that says, "Look at me, Ma!" Raja was nine months old then, clinging to furniture while tentatively teaching himself the fine art of walking. He had been on formula for about a month and had been eating solid food for two months longer. He was the epitome of health; never had an ear infection and always had a pleasant demeanor. Except for the colic that kept him crying four hours every night, he was a model infant. At 32-years old, I had never wanted anything like I wanted my son. He is my only child. I love him with an intensity that I have never before felt.

When I became pregnant, I made a solemn vow before God and my unborn son that I would do everything possible to create opportunities for him to have a beautiful life. Of course, that meant birthing him without medication and raising him with as much love and wisdom as possible. Like most parents, I read every book I could get my hands on, memorizing the first-year developmental milestones. Raja was right on track and I was radiant with joy. I was staying at home to raise my son. I didn't want to miss a thing.

Raja didn't want me to miss a thing either. He woke up every 90 minutes from the day he was born, nursing and falling asleep to awaken 90 minutes later. Exhausted, I called the pediatrician when Raja was ten days old to inquire about his waking frequency. The pediatrician assured me it would even out, but it didn't. Looking back, it was a sign of infantile autism, but this was never mentioned to me, nor would I have suspected it. After all, I knew a little about autism from my college psychology classes. Raja's behavior did not match the despondent and reclusive symptoms I had seen in films. Raja was warm and responsive, engaging in simple games with glee, enjoying attention and encouragement while he performed new feats. No, it would take an additional 16 months for Raja to *begin* distancing himself from strangers, as autism's insidious assault slowly began chipping away at the charming toddler Raja had become.

Just after Raja's first birthday, I sold my home and moved to be near Raja's father and paternal grandparents. Although Raja's father had left when Raja was two weeks old, he re-emerged when Raja was ten months old, stating that he and his parents wanted involvement. We spent Christmas together. I closed on the sale of my home in January. Raja and I moved to an apartment five minutes from their home.

Raja's father and paternal grandparents ate much differently than we did and Raja enjoyed visiting Grandma and Grandpa's house as much for the food as the company. They ate a steady diet of prepackaged and frozen foods, hardly ever eating vegetables. Snacks such as pretzels and chips were readily available, as well as frozen treats and Grandpa's candy stash. Moreover, they ate quite a bit of pizza and fast food, opting for one or the other three or more times a week. Gradually, Raja stopped eating vegetables at home, then omitted beans and most fruit. Adding to a growing list of autistic symptoms of which I was unaware, Raja was self-limiting his diet. Eventually, he reduced his diet to a predictable handful of foods usually containing starch, sugar, dairy products, or flour.

Due to the close proximity and newness of the relationship, Raja spent a considerable time at Grandma and Grandpa's house. One evening, they brought Raja home and he was observably different, both physically and in demeanor. Raja had been walking for two months and had gained considerable balance and coordination for his age. However, this evening he was wobbly and uncoordinated, acting like one who was tipsy from drinking alcohol. Since I knew their home was alcohol-free, I ruled out the possibility that Raja had inadvertently sipped some spirits, but remained perplexed nonetheless. I watched as Raja stumbled and fell, giddy and sloppy, laughing all the while. I inquired why Raja was behaving this way and was told they did not know. I grabbed my camera and took a photo of him, watching and waiting to see what would happen. Within several hours the symptoms subsided and never appeared again.

About a month later, I developed the roll of film and had the photo enlarged. Upon close inspection, I was aghast to see Raja looking slightly mentally retarded, with droopy, red eyes and an unfocused gaze. In the picture, Raja's pupils are quite dilated, his eyes are puffy, and the skin around his cheeks and chin is red and bumpy. Looking back, this incident was the first indication of a food allergy. At the time, however, I had no idea that food could manifest such profound changes and dismissed it because the symptoms disappeared and never returned. Tragically, I did not know that Raja's mental and physical manifestations were indications of an allergic response and that repetitive allergic responses could result in diagnosable autism. Raja was 14 months old when this incident occurred. In my ignorance, Raja continued eating his self-limited diet while undetected autism slowly dismantled his emerging social, cognitive, and physical capabilities.

Nearing his second birthday, Raja had no language except an occasional word that he uttered once and never repeated. We had befriended a lovely family with a son who was almost Raja's age and our sons spent a lot of time together, giving me an opportunity to compare Raja with a developmental peer. At the time we met, Raja's friend, Michael, had not been talking either. Well-meaning friends and family had told Michael's parents what they said to me, "Don't worry, boys are slower than girls." Yet, even Michael was beginning to speak before turning two and he delighted in trying to say new words. Raja, on the other hand, did not. When we took Raja's wagon to the park, Michael always wanted to pull it; Raja never did. Additionally, Raja did not usually want to go to Michael's house and did not reciprocate the enthusiasm that Michael showed in playing with "Ra-ra." Although this was puzzling, I hoped that Raja's disinterest in Michael was somehow connected with a disinterest in parallel play.

However, suspicions that something was wrong were beginning to sprout. Apparently they had sprouted in my neighbors also, for at least four of them had come to my apartment one day to tell me not to worry that Raja was not talking. Separately, they had watched a television program the night before that profiled late-talkers; the language delay in these children was due to genius. This event was memorable to me, because it was actually my first tip-off that my neighbors had been paying attention to Raja and had noticed something in his behavior—probably besides lack of language—that was not like other children his age.

Within two weeks of each other, Michael and his family moved out of state and Raja and I moved to a small college town where I could finish my degree. Settling in, I looked for play groups that Raja and I might join, but couldn't find any. Finally, I called the county help line, which connected me with the program director for first-borns. The director confirmed that there were no play groups in town but welcomed me to join her first-born group. She said the children were much younger than Raja, who was 31-months old by then, but encouraged us to come anyway, so we did.

As we entered the small room crammed with moms and toddlers, Raja's reaction was typical: he clung to me for dear life and did not want to play, no matter how I coaxed or encouraged him. He was not interested in the toys that were there and I did not invest much time trying to interest him as he was not interested in his toys at home.

Casually observing his interaction, the program director asked me questions about Raja. Before the play session ended, she suggested I take him to see a pediatrician for a full physical. I stated that I wanted the best in town; she said that would be her husband. Upon leaving the cramped room, we walked to the reception desk and made an appointment for a full physical with the program director's husband.

The doctor had a lovely, gentle demeanor and a nonchalant way of referring us to a local program that would evaluate Raja for language delay. Later that day, I called the number on the prescription slip and made an appointment to meet with the Special Needs Coordinator the following week. Arriving at the facility, the coordinator welcomed us and asked questions regarding Raja and his lack of language. She suggested Raja be evaluated by a team of specialists to determine the seriousness of his language delay. She indicated the team was excellent with children, saying they worked hard to make children feel comfortable. After a lengthy discussion, we made an appointment for a developmental evaluation two weeks later.

Those two weeks were wrought with fear and conflicted feelings. I had no experience with child specialists except pediatricians and the pediatricians we had seen had never spent any more time with us than was absolutely necessary to perform a physical evaluation. Now, four people whom I had never met were going to evaluate my son's developmental progress and their opinions would become part of his permanent medical record. What if they were wrong? Would they really be able to appreciate Raja as a person and treat him with dignity, or would they make him perform a battery of tests designed to measure how quickly he would fail? Moreover, I wanted Raja to do his very best, not to impress the experts, but because I wanted an accurate idea of where he was in relation to other children his age—at least as accurate as could be determined in artificial testing circumstances.

Quickly, two weeks passed and the morning of the evaluation had arrived. There was no way to "prepare" Raja for the test except to make sure he had a good night's rest, a hearty breakfast, and some "outside time" before we met the team at the county health office. Raja was in good spirits. I was trying to be brave as I took his hand and led him into the building, hearing the sound of my heart beating hard in my ears.

The team was comprised of four professionals—a pediatrician, a cognitive therapist, a physical therapist, and a speech therapist—and I have nothing but the highest praise for them. They worked beautifully with Raja, smoothly transitioning him from one activity to the next, working alone, in pairs, or as a trio, while the one who was not working with Raja asked me non-stop questions. Raja enjoyed them, and they him, extending our testing time beyond the normal three hours because we were having such a good time. We broke for lunch. When we reconvened, they sat as a team and took turns discussing their evaluation of Raja using their individual professional perspectives, giving me ample opportunities to ask questions and clarify concepts.

They said Raja was an enigma; they had never seen a child like him. He had performed higher than normal on some tests and lower than normal on others. They stated that Raja was developmentally delayed. They suggested that we wait a year and perform another evaluation at that time. They also believed that Raja would benefit from therapies and suggested that we enroll in cognitive, physical, occupational, and speech therapy as soon as possible. I thanked them profusely for their kindness and complimented them on their abilities. I was very proud of Raja for acting so naturally in a foreign setting. I looked forward to reading the formal, written evaluation that would be mailed to me in 30 days and happily drove us home.

As my liaison, the Special Needs Coordinator was present at the conclusion of the evaluation when the team was reporting their findings to me. It was her job to record the team's recommendations, as well as to briefly inform me that she and I would be meeting at a later date when she would handle the appointments for therapies. When she came to my home to help me choose therapies and make appointments, she presented me with a chart prepared by the evaluation team that I had not received before. The chart indicated the team's assessment of Raja's developmental progress and showed, in bold detail, the age-related numbers they felt best represented Raja's capabilities at the time of testing.

When I received the chart I felt as if I had been stabbed in my very soul, looking at numbers almost *two years younger* than Raja's chronological age. The team charted Raja's language skills as those of a 12-month old and his self-help skills as those of an 18-month old. Choking back the tears, I reminded the coordinator that the team said Raja had performed higher than normal on some tasks and that the chart did not reflect that information. She apologized, saying that the team should have given me the chart during the evaluation. She explained that the numbers represented the average of the highs and lows Raja scored during testing; that she was merely the messenger, not the interpreter. Whatever else we talked about regarding therapies and scheduling appointments was a total blur. She excused herself. I bawled my eyes out for four hours straight.

Raja was three months shy of his third birthday. I had been looking forward to placing him in a great pre-school program where he would be nourished mentally, emotionally, and socially. I envisioned that pre-school would prepare him for a fabulous private school which I had investigated and anticipated since he was in the womb. I had been looking forward to going back to work part-time and completing my degree at the local university. Not only were these visions fixed in my mind, they were also part of the beautiful life I sought to create for us! Sob by sob, my version of the beautiful life was draining away, replaced by the memory of the pact I made with God and Raja when I was pregnant. No matter what, whether Raja was severely deformed or extremely retarded, I wanted this baby with all my might and would do everything in my willpower to love him as fully as any person could. Each tear brought me closer to that vow. At the end of four hours I was done crying. I would stand by my son and do everything I could for him, praying for guidance every step of the way.

Raja's evaluation was completed a few weeks before Thanksgiving. We had made arrangements to spend the holiday with my dear friend, Marina, and her lovely family. We had not seen Marina in nearly two years and I was looking forward to visiting. Moreover, Marina knew about Raja's evaluation and wanted to see him for herself. Marina and her husband, Rob, picked us up at the airport. We spent three glorious weeks soaking up Marina's much-missed company and conversation.

Marina is both extremely kind and resourceful; her interest in Raja was non-stop. She watched him with a compassionate intensity, taking in everything he did, making silent and verbal comparisons with the developmental markers her children had passed at certain ages. We discussed Raja's language delay and that the onset of language is organic, not learned. We agreed that the development of language is not need-oriented and that Raja's language deficit did not result from me meeting all his needs and alleviating his need to talk. Instead, we believed that a child communicates out of interest and that speaking is as natural as the desire to play. Through observation and conversation, we concluded that Raja's language deficit and peculiar behaviors had a physiological foundation but did not yet understand its origins.

Every day Marina would take her observations to the street, discussing Raja's behaviors with other parents to gather information in our search for understanding. She would bring her children home and report to me what she had learned in conversation with other parents on the playground, at piano recitals, or after church services. One day she came home and shared a report that I knew was truth as soon as she spoke it. She had been describing Raja's behavior to a parent who said the descriptions reminded her of her brother who has Asperger's syndrome, which is a form of autism. Instantly, chills went up my arms. "That's it," I said, and we sat together in silence, relieved to connect Raja's behaviors with a known disorder, nervous to know what autism really meant. Wasting no time, Rob immediately accessed the Internet, retrieving information ranging from criteria used for diagnosis to a nationwide list of support groups. We were finally on our way.

Raja and I returned home. Trembling, I called the evaluation team facilitator to obtain her opinion regarding Raja's possible autism. We engaged in a long conversation in which she stated that she did not think Raja was autistic. When I pointed out the diagnostic criteria for autism and how closely Raja's behavior matched this criterion, she suggested that Raja might outgrow these behaviors and that she did not want me to put a label like autism on him. Over and over, she tried to dissuade me from scheduling an autism evaluation but I could not see any logic in this. I kept sensing that therapies for autistic children differ dramatically from therapies for developmentally delayed children. I did not want Raja to undergo a year of inappropriate therapy when we could have used our time and resources more wisely. We ended the conversation in disagreement. I thanked her for her time, then scheduled Raja for an evaluation at an autism diagnosis center.

There was a seven-month waiting list for an autistic evaluation, so I made the best use of this time by completing my bachelor's degree, joining a special needs parents' support group, and researching what was known about autism. Specifically, I was looking for a medical explanation or therapeutic approach that sought to understand autism on the organic level. I talked to everyone I could and pursued every path that held some promise, including supplements, parasite detoxification, and Nambudripad's Allergy Elimination Techniques (N.A.E.T treatments). Even my college acquaintances were gathering information for me. As the semester was nearly over, a dear friend handed me a photocopy of an article that appeared in *Parents* magazine, entitled, "We Cured Our Son of Autism." As I delved into the article, I could tell that the mother who was telling her son's story was a kindred soul. In 18 months, this mother restored her son to normally developing status using an organic approach called the casein-free, gluten-free diet.

Additionally, the footnote at the end of the article referenced a resource book written by a parent of an autistic son for other parents wishing to implement the diet, *Special Diets For Special Kids*. At long last, my prayer for help was answered.

Completing my degree required child-care for Raja. While child-care normally consisted of two three-hour visits per week, I was fortunate to have a friend stay during finals, providing child-care for Raja and study time for me. While my head was buried in books, Raja ate a steady diet of cereal, sandwiches, and crackers—things he usually ate infrequently and only in small quantities. By the time I had taken my last final, Raja had become aggressive and unable to attend to anything. He was unable to focus, listen, or process a request, and slapped or kicked when he was asked to do something he did not want to do. The final straw was when he lay down on the floor in a department store, which he had not done in nearly a year. Suddenly, I connected his behavior with his diet and knew what had to be done. Leaving the department store in haste, I drove home knowing I would immediately discard every scrap of food that did not conform to the casein-free, gluten-free diet.

12 full grocery bags later, I surveyed the kitchen and was amazed to see that only two acceptable foods remained: fish and rice. So began our elimination diet, eating fish and rice for every meal until Raja appeared to reach and maintain a stable state. 14 days later, in his new, stable state, I met Raja—a boy I used to know before losing two years to autism. Tears of joy, relief, and sorrow flowed as Raja took the keys from my hand to lock the front door when we were leaving the house—a milestone he had achieved but had not repeated in a year and a half. How time stands still for one in the clutches of autism!

Like other stories of autistic children, Raja had experienced many appropriate developmental milestones; then, without explanation, began drifting away. Raja's debilitation was so slow that it was hard to identify. The clues were so subtle that I rationalized them as personality traits belonging to an only child. Additionally, the physical symptoms that cropped up seemed unrelated. It was not until I suspected that Raja had autism (prior to diagnosis) that the seemingly unrelated symptoms found a paradigm to which they belonged.

We traveled to the diagnostic center for Raja's autistic evaluation in June. Again, trepidation made my heart pound. We had had a negative experience with an audiologist at a university-affiliated program whose insensitivity toward Raja was a lesson for me. Sadly, not all professionals working with special needs kids treat them with the courtesy, dignity, and understanding I expected, so I now entered testing situations as Raja's open-minded advocate, willing to listen and participate in reasonable activities, yet ready to strenuously object at the first sign of unkind treatment. To their credit, the staff was very courteous and flexible, treating Raja with dignity and meeting him at his level. Four hours later, they gently broke the news that Raja is autistic, which made official the goose bumps I felt at Marina's house.

Raja and I began the early version of Comprehensive Organic Intervention two weeks prior to his autistic diagnosis using the casein-free, gluten-free diet outlined in the book *Special Diets For Special Kids*. We implemented the casein-free, gluten-free diet nine months ago, and through refinement based on observation, research, and experimentation, formulated Comprehensive Organic Intervention. Using Comprehensive Organic Intervention, Raja has made outstanding progress.

Within the first two weeks of making dietary changes, Raja reached a stable state, in which he could listen, attend to, and execute requests with minimal repetition on my part. Once he achieved a stable state, Raja began asserting his knowledge and independence with actions indicating developmental gain (such as taking the keys from my hand and placing them in the front door lock when we were leaving the house). Within three months, Raja was no longer afraid of children, eagerly joining in games and play. He began using some language and imitating animal sounds. He knew how old he was and could indicate this by holding up the appropriate number of fingers. He developed fine motor skills and could easily maneuver the computer mouse and button to play games with occasional help. He began sleeping uninterrupted for up to four hours, waking without panicking and screaming.

In the next three months, Raja's attention span normalized and his language expanded. He began dressing and undressing himself. His eye contact improved. He was able to potty train in two weeks once we avoided all forms of sugar. He was no longer startled by loud noises and began enjoying music and dance. His uninterrupted sleep continued improving and he awoke without distress even if I was not right beside him.

In the last three months, Raja's language has exploded. He now talks constantly. He is speaking in six-word sentences and can verbalize most needs and requests. His enunciation steadily improves and he speaks new words daily. He knows all the letters of the alphabet and can count to 20 unaided. He knows my name and can spell his. He can identify emotions based on facial expressions. He chooses and loads his computer games without assistance, telling me about his favorite sequences. Raja's recovery continues every day. His developmental abilities are catching up with his chronological age.

While Raja's developmental gain remains paramount, the most exiting result of his recovery has been his emerging personality. For the first time, I have met my son as a growing and multifaceted individual. I am finding he is a very gentle and fun-loving soul. Rather than one-sided communication designed to interpret and meet his highly fluctuating and incomprehensible needs, we now talk, smile, and laugh with each other, enjoying the ability to interact. It used to be difficult for Raja to interact with other children because they expected him to participate in verbal exchanges and social rituals like taking turns. Now it is exciting to watch him navigate the uncertain waters of sharing and playing, taking his rightful place beside his peers.

Raja's recovery has allowed me to graduate from a caregiver to a mom. I am privileged to experience him as a whole human being, reveling in his perceptions, accomplishments, and need for discipline. No longer concerned about unexpected noises that would terrorize him, I am becoming relaxed. Once very sleep deprived, I now sleep uninterrupted and awaken feeling refreshed. I am even convinced that the miracle of Raja's speech is not going to disappear and have stopped holding my breath when he talks.

Lately I have been reviving dismissed dreams and renewing hopes that had once vanished in tears of grief and sorrow. I find myself thinking about educational environments that provide social, emotional, and intellectual nourishment. I muse about train trips, swimming with dolphins, and a week at Disney World. I reflect on the boy I am discovering as my son and imagine the man he will be. Raja's recovery has been my recovery, too. We are climbing out of autism, and into the realm of possibilities, one bite at a time. With his arms wrapped around me, I look into Raja's smiling eyes and cannot imagine it getting any better than this. I am convinced that the beautiful life is not as far off as I once believed it to be.

Step One:
Documentation

It would be hard to say too much about the role thorough and accurate documentation plays in facilitating your child's recovery and developmental gain. Comprehensive Organic Intervention relies on documentation to track relationships between dietary and environmental influences and the reactions they elicit in your child. Documentation provides a record of your child's progress, allowing you to alter his dietary and environmental influences to maximize developmental gain. Implementing a thorough and accurate documentation system is the first step in securing your child's recovery. Please initiate this step before commencing the dietary and environmental changes outlined in the following chapters. It is necessary to document present conditions before implementing Comprehensive Organic Intervention.

Begin by purchasing a journal that provides adequate space to record detailed information—any spiral-bound notebook should suffice. Entitle your notebook, "Food and Reaction Journal." Use the Food and Reaction Journal to record observations and information related to your child. Time and date each entry, recording the type and approximate amount of food and drink your child consumes. Make one journal entry per snack, meal, or drink. Additionally, describe your impressions of your child's physical, mental, emotional, social, and behavioral conditions. Include sleep patterns, duration and extent of hypersensitivity, and manifestations of anti-social activity. Record all observations, even if every day is basically the same. Be honest. Describe your observations in detail.

Use the Food and Reaction Journal every day to record the information listed above. You will continue recording your observations in the Food and Reaction Journal once Comprehensive Organic Intervention commences. It will become an invaluable tool thereafter.

Recordation in the Food and Reaction Journal creates a tracking device for your child's progress. Tracking your child's dietary and environmental reactions allows his individual profile to surface, creating opportunities for greater refinement. Implementing refinements protects your child's homeostasis, or stable state. Maintaining a stable state is the key ingredient in your child's recovery and the second step in Comprehensive Organic Intervention. We will now turn our attention to Step Two: Achieving a Stable State.

Step Two:
Achieving A Stable State

Achieving a stable state is the primary goal of Comprehensive Organic Intervention because it is during the maintenance of a stable state that recovery and developmental gain occur. A stable state is one in which your child attains observable cognitive and behavioral equilibrium, empowering you to become his ally in promoting developmental gain. A stable state provides a cognitive and behavioral baseline by which you can gauge your child's reactions to dietary and environmental factors. Achieving and maintaining a stable state is critical to the success of this program. It is the vehicle that will empower you to take corrective measures when dietary or environmental influences provoke reactions.

A stable state is achieved using an elimination diet, which will be discussed in detail later. Presently, we will explore the concept and experience of a stable state. Although your child's experience may vary, it is probable that the creation of a stable state will return him to one or more of the last developmental milestones he passed before autism took him off course. I offer this passage as background to help you familiarize yourself with the concept and experience of achieving a stable state.

Raja achieved a stable state within two weeks of maintaining an elimination diet. In a stable state, Raja's personality and demeanor became calm. He was able to listen and follow through with an ease that I had forgotten. I did not have to tell him 12-20 times that we were going to get in our Jeep, only to carry him to the Jeep anyway. I was able to tell him 1-5 times that we were going to the Jeep and he responded appropriately. He stopped what he was doing and proceeded toward the front door. He took the keys from my hand and waited outside the front door to place the key in the lock. He locked the house before leaving. He then proceeded to the Jeep where he used the key in the lock to gain entrance. Did this level of equilibrium mean Raja was no longer autistic? Unfortunately, not. However, it meant that the creation of a stable state allowed Raja to pick up where he left off developmentally—before autism unraveled his choices and behaviors. It also established a baseline against which all behavioral and cognitive assessments could be measured, taking corrective action to return to a stable state, if necessary.

A stable state is reached when your child exhibits behaviorally measurable tendencies that vary little in degree marked by sustained, positive changes in demeanor. Additionally, your child may exhibit the enhanced ability to respond more normally in typical circumstances with familiar people. In other words, you will know it when you see it because it feels easier and calmer than usual. In Raja's case, the changes were behaviorally and cognitively measurable, demonstrated by his ability to listen, respond appropriately, and express an interest in his surroundings. In a stable state, the level of calm and ease may be subtle but it is there. When the calm and ease is sustained with little variance, it is a stable state. Achieving and maintaining a stable state is the primary goal of Comprehensive Organic Intervention.

Recognition of a stable state is critical to the success of this approach. When you recognize that your child has entered a stable state, saturate yourself with images and sensations associated with your child's behavior and cognition. Study your child, memorizing every aspect of his equilibrium. Maintain the conditions facilitating a stable state until you are certain you will recognize its interruption. The behavioral and cognitive changes achieved in a stable state will be particular to your child and may be subtle, so close attention is warranted. When you are confident you can identify a stable state, you will also be ready to identify the interruption of a stable state, called a reaction. When you can identify a stable state or a reaction, you are ready to proceed. Do not proceed before you are ready.

Symptoms of a Reaction

Once your child has successfully achieved and maintained a stable state using dietary intervention, detecting a reaction becomes a possibility. I know Raja is having a reaction when he does one or more of the following: enters a mental stupor; becomes hyperactive; becomes hypersensitive to sounds, smells, or touch; does not listen or follow directions; has dilated pupils; has unusual thirst; has restless sleep patterns; exhibits increased tic-like behavior; exhibits a temporary language deficit; exhibits subtle or overt anti-social behavior; attention span diminishes; eye contact diminishes; may not respond to his name; becomes demanding; becomes fixated on objects; becomes aggressive; exhibits tactile defensiveness; appears stiff and disjointed; becomes clumsy; seems unusually giddy or happy; becomes manic about a particular food.

Once Raja achieved and maintained a stable state, his recovery has been, and remains, very steady. In a stable state, Raja makes developmental gain that has measurably increased over time. Often, Raja seems to make developmental gain daily. In addition to the aforementioned symptoms, a lack of steadily increasing developmental gain also indicates a reaction. *Any time Raja's developmental gain has seemingly hit a plateau, I suspect a reaction.*

A reaction, then, can range from very subtle symptoms to overt physical manifestations that make your child hard to control. The symptoms of reaction your child will manifest will be particular to him.

However, it is important to realize that a reaction is manifest anytime your child deviates from a stable state. Once your child has started achieving measurable developmental gain, he is also manifesting symptoms of a reaction if his developmental gain appears to reach a plateau that lasts seven days or longer. Although developmental gain is not necessarily linear, it is measurable. If, after achieving and maintaining a stable state, your child's developmental gain does not appear to be steadily increasing after seven days, suspect a reaction and take appropriate corrective measures.

We will address what to do when a reaction occurs in Step Four. Presently, we will review the steps to achieving a stable state.

How to Achieve a Stable State

Purchase a journal to be labeled, "Food and Reaction Journal." Document your child's eating habits and record his physical, mental, emotional, social, and behavioral states before commencing the elimination diet.

Choose a start date for the elimination diet, explained in Step Three. The elimination diet is the vehicle for achieving a stable state.

Achieving and maintaining a stable state is the foundation of recovery. A stable state represents homeostasis, a condition that facilitates developmental gain. Maintenance of a stable state is the necessary factor in your child's recovery. Sustained maintenance of a stable state is the goal of this program and the means by which your child will experience developmental gain.

Now that you are acquainted with the role a stable state plays in facilitating your child's recovery, we will examine Step Three: The Elimination Diet.

Step Three:
The Elimination Diet

The elimination diet is the third step in Comprehensive Organic Intervention and the vehicle by which a stable state is achieved. The first purpose of the elimination diet is make recovery possible by achieving and maintaining a stable state. The second purpose is to cleanse the body and cupboards of foods that will no longer be eaten in the promotion of developmental recovery. The structure of the elimination diet is to remove all foods that trigger or exacerbate equilibrium interruptions by selecting and preparing well tolerated foods to achieve and maintain a stable state. The duration of the elimination diet is subjective, dependent on the creation and recognition of a stable state.

Prior to commencing the elimination diet, Raja was muscle tested for food and environmental allergies as part of a treatment strategy we tried before developing Comprehensive Organic Intervention. The allergy test was administered by a licensed Doctor of Oriental Medicine using Nambudripad's Allergy Elimination Techniques (N.A.E.T.). N.A.E.T. testing is a non-invasive method of determining which food and environmental allergens trigger an allergic response. Upon completion, we found that Raja was allergic to almost everything except apples, onions, chicken, beef, fish, seafood, and rice. Although I have not incorporated information gleaned from the N.A.E.T. testing process in the formulation of Comprehensive Organic Intervention, I relate our experience to preserve the integrity of events leading to the creation of this approach.

Raja had been receiving N.A.E.T. treatments twice a month for two months prior to commencing the elimination diet. Although I found the process fascinating, we were not getting the results I had hoped for and started the elimination diet after the episode in the department store. During our elimination diet, we ate only frozen tilapia, uncooked rice, and canola oil that was used for frying. If you are thinking that this sounds harsh, you are right. However, when we emerged from the elimination diet Raja began taking an interest in food he formerly refused and his interest in trying new foods continues to this day. Raja's interest in food is not only a pleasure and relief but a nutritional boost as well. You'd be amazed how good a carrot looks after eating only fish and rice for two weeks!

Raja and I completed the elimination diet together (my husband, Larry, completed the elimination diet separately four weeks later). I chose to complete the diet with Raja because I am half of his genetic makeup, reasoning that I could understand his reactions better if I were experiencing the diet as well. I am glad that I did and would urge you to experience this diet with your child. Completing the diet together offers your support to your child and gives you a unique opportunity to experience the power in food. I discovered that food has the ability to harm as well as heal and that certain substances are truly addictive. Withdrawals were my body's way of bargaining with me, attempting to make me miserable enough that I felt driven to consume the substance I was craving. Additionally, I could speculate with some degree of certainty regarding what was happening when Raja's behavior indicated he was experiencing withdrawals. I did not have any expectations in completing the diet with Raja; it was just something I felt compelled to do in supporting him. However, completing the elimination diet together brought us closer and returned to me a level of vitality I had lost around ninth grade.

Regarding withdrawals, Raja and I experienced withdrawal symptoms on the fourth day of the elimination diet. Raja would be happy then suddenly cry for no apparent reason. This alternated throughout the day. I had a headache off and on and had a tremendous urge to eat sweets. By the fifth day, however, there were no more immediate withdrawal symptoms. The length and type of withdrawals may depend on the individual or may not be experienced at all. In retrospect, I think we might have diminished the intensity of our withdrawals by drinking more water. I would boost water intake at the first sign of discomfort or craving to see if symptoms can be ameliorated.

Considerations for an Elimination Diet

A good starting point for an elimination diet is to choose neutral protein and vegetable sources that do not cause reactions and drink only purified water. Appropriate foods will be wholesome and the preparation simple—home cooked the same way every time without salt, pepper, seasonings, or condiments of any kind. Additionally, the food must be the same food regardless of the meal. In other words, Raja and I ate fish and rice every single day for every meal for two weeks. The only beverage we drank was purified water. It is necessary to clean out all the cupboards and the refrigerator and freezer, keeping therein only those things that conform to the diet. Your child may frequently go to the cupboards and refrigerator looking for food, eating what is there. You want to be certain he does not eat food that is not on the elimination diet. If he eats even a bite of something that is not on the diet, he will need to remain on the elimination diet an additional week to clear the potential effects of an infraction.

In choosing foods to prepare for the elimination diet, select whole foods that do not provoke a reaction. In determining whether your child is having a reaction, watch for any food he appears addicted to or eats with great enthusiasm or regularity. In Raja's case, he got a certain gleam in his eye that indicated a food was causing a greater-than-normal response. For example, his first bite of plain, cooked noodles had him diving in the noodle bowl at nine months old. Sitting on the kitchen floor, Raja ate cold noodles in huge handfuls right from the refrigerator. At the time, I thought nothing of it, recalling a similar story my father shared with me about my first taste of ice cream. However, I look back now and realize that Raja's heightened interest in noodles was very different from any other food he had tasted at that time. He ate other food calmly, without fuss, but became manic over noodles. As parents, we recognize our children's unusual responses to foods. Whether your child becomes manic or exhibits a different form of excitement unique to a particular food, immediately remove it from the diet and find a substitute the does not elicit excitement.

Over the course of experimenting with Raja's diet and documenting his reactions, I have found that protein is the mainstay of his equilibrium. When starting the elimination diet, choose a protein source such as fish, fowl or meat that your child likes but that does not elicit an allergic reaction. An ideal choice would be one that your child does not eat frequently but will eat when served, such as rabbit or venison. You will find suggestions for the elimination diet at the end of this chapter. It is imperative that all food remain pure and wholesome, making it necessary to read labels carefully. Stay away from processed meat such as ground meat or fowl, lunch meat, hot dogs, bacon, or sausage, and any whole fish, fowl or meat that contains natural flavorings. Choose only foods that have not been adulterated in any way and read labels carefully to be safe.

In choosing a vegetable for the elimination diet, I suggest yucca root. Due to lack of exposure, yucca root is unlikely to produce an allergic reaction and has a pleasant, mild taste. It is simple to prepare (peel, core, boil, and mash) and is widely available in the produce section of most supermarkets.

Regarding beverages, drink and cook with only purified water. We use a PUR water filter that attaches to the faucet and has replaceable filters. It is easy to use without being very cumbersome. It removes lead, bacteria, and chlorine from our water. A water filter is a good investment because you will also be drinking and cooking with purified water after the elimination diet, which helps reduce the number and types of toxins entering your child's system.

Even though we ate vast quantities of rice during our elimination diet experience, I would suggest eating yucca root rather than rice to eliminate potential reactions to rice. Be certain to eat protein for breakfast and have yucca root, if desired. Starting the day with protein appears to stabilize blood sugar and eliminates dramatic mood swings.

Suggestions For An Elimination Diet

Protein—beef, chicken, turkey, fish, or exotic game without flavorings, additives, preservatives, derivatives, coloring, etc. Choose one source of protein and use it continuously for the duration of the diet. If possible, buy range fed meat that is free from hormones and antibiotics (this may require buying meat at a meat market or in the butcher section of a health food store). Do not buy ground meat or fowl or pre-formed burgers as these may contain hidden gluten in the form of fillers or "natural flavorings" even if the label indicates the product is pure. Read labels carefully. Use whole products to be certain of purity. When in doubt, ask or avoid. Cook with pure canola or olive oil, if necessary. Do not add any seasonings.

Yucca Root—peel, core, boil, and mash. Can be thinned or whipped (like mashed potatoes) using purified water or pure canola or olive oil.

Frying or baking—purified water or pure canola or olive oil only.

Drink purified water only.

If your child is unusually interested in eating the foods you are using on the elimination diet, suspect a reaction and replace the food immediately. Like water, food is largely a neutral substance. While you do not want your child to go hungry, he will be experiencing a dramatic shift in how he relates to food during this time. Any unusual attraction to a food may be an indication of food allergy. Make substitutions and observe.

There is a long list of things to avoid and I have sought to simplify the elimination diet by including only that which is acceptable. However, in the interest of being fully informed, here are a few additional guidelines of foods to avoid.

Avoid: All common allergens, including food containing, or derived from, yeast, milk, wheat, soy, corn, gluten, casein, eggs, sugar, chocolate, salt, and nuts. Avoid all spices, seasonings, condiments, and sauce or gravy mixes. Avoid all prepackaged foods, such as food that is wrapped, boxed, bottled, canned, frozen, pre-baked or pre-cooked. Avoid anything containing additives, derivatives, preservatives, waxes, flavorings, flavor enhancers (such as monosodium glutamate), coloring, dyes, sweeteners, pesticides, and other chemicals. Avoid all processed food. Avoid all convenience foods. Avoid all take-out food. Avoid all restaurant food. Avoid all food that is not prepared at home the same way every time. Avoid the bakery, deli, dairy, baking, cereal, snack, and frozen food sections of the supermarket. For the duration of the elimination diet, avoid fruit in all forms. Avoid all beverages except purified water. Read every label every time. When in doubt, avoid it.

I think the greatest fear regarding an elimination diet is that your child will go hungry because he has self-limited to a handful of foods that you will be removing from his diet, forcing him to eat new foods or starve. As I have indicated in sharing our story, Raja's reaction in the department store was so unusual and pronounced that I did not have time to fear that he would starve on the elimination diet. I simply went home and cleaned out our cupboards, convicted that we would eat whatever acceptable foods remained.

Early in the course of our elimination diet, Raja went to the refrigerator and cupboards numerous times a day looking for something to eat besides fish and rice. Every time he did, I would patiently explain that fish and rice was all we had to eat, opening all the cupboards to show him they were bare. When Raja went looking for food I would offer him some fish and rice, but he refused unless genuinely hungry.

Within three days of commencing the diet, Raja became quiescent when he realized there was nothing in the house to eat but fish and rice. Once he knew we were only eating fish and rice, he went along with the program. What choice did he have? He was hungry and we had only fish and rice to eat, so we ate fish and rice. Raja liked fish, so a diet of fish and rice was an easy adjustment. Ironically, I found that this was one instance where Raja's ability to establish routine was very helpful. Once he understood we were only eating fish and rice at every meal, he fell in line rather quickly and forgot about wanting other food.

I would strongly advise staying out of the grocery store for the duration of the elimination diet if possible. Perhaps you could have your spouse or a friend do your marketing. If that is not possible, try to buy what you need in advance and avoid grocery shopping for at least the first week. For me, the smell of fresh baked goods wafting from the bakery was tough to endure. For Raja, it was difficult to pass the aisles where I used to select a treat to eat while we shopped. Passing by food we used to eat while shopping was a big adjustment. However, I found that my consistent refusals to buy Raja the treat he expected, coupled with attempts to refocus his attention, resulted in a gradual tapering of requests. Eventually, they were eliminated altogether.

Please bear in mind that the purpose of the elimination diet is to eat in the purest state possible while still providing nutrition for daily living. Do not use even a dash of salt, pepper, spices, condiments, sauces, dressings, dairy products, flour products, or anything from the list of foods to avoid. It is imperative to remain 100% faithful to the diet at all times. If an infraction occurs, remain on the diet an additional seven days. Be certain the stable state is achieved and maintained for a sufficient duration that you feel confident in recognizing the signs of a reaction. When you are confident that you will recognize the signs of reaction, you are ready to proceed to Step Four: Ending the Elimination Diet.

Step Four:
Ending the Elimination Diet

Ending the elimination diet signals the beginning of a new lifestyle designed to promote normalcy and developmental achievement through dietary and environmental intervention. The purpose of ending the elimination diet is to expand your child's diet by determining the foods he can tolerate without a reaction. A reaction is any subtle or apparent disruption in your child's equilibrium. A reaction signals an allergy, or immune response, to a food or ingredient. As Dr. Peter D'Adamo describes in *Eat Right For Your Type*,

> Food allergies are not digestive problems. They are immune system reactions to certain foods. Your immune system literally creates an antibody that fights the intrusion of food into your system (pg. 58).

All reactions are negative, hindering recovery and developmental gain. Any food that produces even a slight reaction in your child's physical, mental, emotional, behavioral, or social disposition should be eliminated immediately. Your goal in ending the elimination diet is to expand your child's food choices to the fullest by including only foods that do not produce reactions.

When a Reaction Occurs

A reaction is a disruption in your child's stable state. A reaction includes any atypical physical, mental, emotional, social, or behavioral manifestation. Reactions may include "happy" disruptions, such as laughing, giggling, giddiness, or physical clumsiness that your child considers funny. Such "happy" reactions are usually accompanied by an inability to listen and respond appropriately or to curb inappropriate or unwanted behavior when asked. Reactions may also include behaviors and dispositions that make it hard to direct or interact with your child, such as aggressive or anti-social behavior. Any behavior or disposition that deviates from your child's recognizable stable state is a reaction.

When a reaction occurs, identify the offending food immediately. Reinstate the elimination diet plus any other well tolerated foods for one week. After one week, begin introducing foods one at a time. Wait one week before introducing a new food. Continue to drink only purified water.

Considerations in Ending the Elimination Diet

Introduce foods one at a time, for one week, and closely observe potential reactions.

Continue to drink only purified water.

Continue daily documentation in the Food and Reaction Journal.

Introduce food constituents one at a time, for one week, on foods that you have tested and are well tolerated. For example, test herbs and spices one at a time on foods that produce no reaction in your child. Test each herb and spice individually for one week. If a reaction occurs, follow the instructions above.

If an infraction inadvertently occurs (e.g., if your child accidentally eats something he is not supposed to), consider it a reaction and follow the instructions above.

In order to end the elimination diet and introduce a wider variety of foods, it will be necessary to detail general guidelines regarding what can and cannot be eaten. We will now explore Step Five: Food and Ingredients to Avoid.

Step Five:
Food And Ingredients To Avoid

The goal of this diet is to choose foods that do not produce reactions while creating a broad base of foods that are well tolerated. To accomplish this goal, it is necessary to identify foods and ingredients that are likely to cause reactions in order to avoid them. In this chapter, we will examine common culprits in food-induced reactions. A quick-reference sheet is provided at the end of the chapter for your convenience.

Casein

Casein is the protein present in cows' milk. Casein is present in milk and milk-based products, such as any product you would find in the dairy section, any prepared food containing a dairy product, and even in soy-based dairy products such as soy cheese. In certain instances, such as soy cheese, casein is listed as an ingredient on the food label. In other cases, such as milk and dairy products, casein is not listed on the label as a separate ingredient since it is intrinsic to the food itself.

Casein is a powerful and insidious allergen, responsible for inducing reactions. In the book, *Fighting For Tony*, author Mary Callahan notes that casein was responsible for causing a cerebral allergic reaction in her infant son, Tony. Tony's cerebral allergy resulted in autistic behaviors to the degree that he was eventually diagnosed with autism. Tony's symptoms disappeared when his parents removed products containing casein from his diet. Over time, Tony recovered from diagnosable autism.

Casein is always present in dairy products. Look for casein listed as an ingredient on mock dairy products such as soy and rice milk, cheese, or ice cream. Avoid all dairy products and mock dairy products containing casein.

Gluten

Gluten is the protein found in grains. Gluten is present in wheat, oats, barley, rye, and triticale, and is believed to be present in einkorn, semolina, bulgar, kamut, durum, and spelt. Gluten is thus present in every type of commercially produced bread and cereal product, including bread, oatmeal, muffins, bagels, pizza, pasta, crackers, and cereal. Gluten may be a hidden ingredient in other foods, such as raisins and dates, as processing machinery is dusted with flour to keep products from sticking. Gluten, in the form of flour, is also a common ingredient in many ground spices as it is used to keep them from caking. Additionally, many products contain gluten derivatives that should also be avoided. A partial list appears below.

Grain vinegar	Curry powder	Malt	Malt syrup
Grain starches	Mustard	Flavorings	Malt flavorings
Grain alcohol	Maltodextrin	Ketchup	Vegetable broth
Cinnamon	Soy sauce	Oat gum	Horseradish
Modified food starch			
Hydrolyzed vegetable protein			

Like casein, gluten is a powerful allergen and is the culprit in the digestive disorder called celiac disease. As diagnosed celiac Bette Hagman says in her excellent cookbook *The Gluten-free Gourmet Cooks Fast And Healthy,* "Celiac disease, or gluten-sensitive enteropathy, is an autoimmune reaction causing damage to the small intestine, usually leading to malnutrition and its consequences" (pg. 9). Additionally, many symptoms mirror those typical of autistic children, including developmental delays (pg. 13). When I read Ms. Hagman's explanation regarding the symptoms of celiac disease, I was surprised to find how many symptoms Raja and other autistic children shared with her description:

> The classic textbook symptoms of the disease in childhood are anemia, failure to grow, behavioral disorders, anorexia {loss of appetite}, and, as the child progresses in the illness, chronic diarrhea {sometimes with fatty, foul-smelling stools that may float}, or, in some cases, severe constipation, some vomiting, and noticeable abdominal distention and/or pain. Not all children present with all or even most of these, and often the diagnosis is delayed because these can be symptoms of other diseases. Dental enamel defects are common in celiac children, but the cause may not be recognized (pg. 12).

It is important to familiarize yourself with gluten and its derivatives so that you may recognize products and situations that your child would do well to avoid. One of the key ways I recognize gluten and its derivatives is to remember that gluten is derived from grains, so that things like grain alcohol, which is common even in herbal tinctures, must be avoided. Keep an eye out for personal care products, such as soap, toothpaste, and shampoos. To the extent possible, avoid over-the-counter medicines as these normally contain a plethora of reactive agents. Watch for natural flavorings in ground meat products. Natural flavorings contain gluten-derivatives and tend to be common in ground turkey and beef.

When you see an ingredient on a label that you do not recognize as being safe for consumption, either do not purchase the item, or purchase it but call the manufacturer before using it. If the manufacturer's representative with whom you speak does not know whether a product contains gluten or its derivatives, return it to the store for a refund. Do not take chances. Even one bite of such a food will trigger a reaction. Reactions mean lost time that cannot be recovered in terms of health and developmental achievement. It is not worth the risk, even to have your child "fit in."

All chemicals and unnaturally occurring ingredients should be avoided as they are likely culprits of food-induced reactions. This includes additives, preservatives, waxes, food coloring, and flavor enhancers. Additionally, food manufacturers are not required to label ingredients used in processing so pre-packaged food should always be suspect. Without labeling, we cannot know what naturally or unnaturally occurring ingredients may be present in pre-packaged food. When in doubt, avoid a product or ingredient to be safe.

Diet and Developmental Gain

In the course of refining Raja's diet to avoid the developmental loss associated with reactions, I have encountered foods and ingredients that have both hampered and increased his developmental gain. Although I do not understand why these relationships exist, dietary refinement is largely responsible for Raja's recovery and rapid developmental gain. Because I believe there is universal applicability among all autistic children, I have outlined the relationships below.

Sugar

We found the following relationships between sugar consumption and developmental gain.

There is no hierarchy of "good" and "bad" types of sugar. Every type of sugar evoked a reaction, including white sugar, brown sugar, turbinado sugar, maple syrup, honey, molasses, glycerin, dried fruit, cooked fruit, frozen fruit, fruit juice, and carrot juice. Even homemade fruit and carrot juice evoked a reaction, as did homemade dried fruit containing no ingredients other than organic fruit.

Any quantity of the aforementioned types of sugar was sufficient to induce a reaction, including as little as a tablespoon in a batch of biscuits.

Reactions include hyperactivity, dilated pupils, inability to focus or concentrate, temporary language deficit, tic-like behavior, tactile defensiveness, physical desensitization, and cognitive impairment. Examples include:

A). During potty training, sugar impacted Raja's physical sensation of having to urinate. After consuming sugar, Raja would urinate and sit in it as though he could not feel that he was engulfed in a puddle of urine. In the absence of sugar, Raja was able to sense his need to urinate and found his potty-chair for appropriate bladder evacuation. When we eliminated sugar altogether, Raja was fully potty trained in two weeks.

B). As Raja's autism progressed, his tactile defensiveness became very pronounced, running and screaming from tooth or hair brushing as well as trimming finger and toe nails. After consuming sugar, Raja would exhibit strenuous objections to all grooming needs. However, once we eliminated sugar altogether, Raja's tactile defensiveness ameliorated.

C). After commencing Comprehensive Organic Intervention for one month, Raja took an interest in his alphabet machine, spending up to 30 minutes per session teaching himself the alphabet. After a few weeks, he was very adept at identifying his letters, indicating correct answers by pressing the right letter. However, after consuming sugar, Raja could not find the letter "g" even after showing him repeatedly. The machine would ask him to identify "g" and he would stare at the keyboard with no comprehension. I would show him "g" as a reminder, but when the machine asked again, he could not remember "g". Once we eliminated sugar, Raja's temporary cognitive impairment ceased immediately, facilitating greater levels of learning.

The most significant relationship noted between sugar intake and impact on developmental gain was that small quantities of whole fruit did not appear to induce reactions or negatively impact developmental gain. For instance, when Raja consumed no more than half a piece of medium-sized fruit during the course of a 24-hour period, he experienced no reaction. However, if he exceeded this amount, or if the fruit of choice was an orange, a reaction occurred. Raja could handle the sugar concentration in whole fruit provided the quantity was closely monitored and the choice of fruit excluded oranges.

Sugar has a pervasive and negative impact on recovery and developmental gain. To maximize your child's recovery and developmental gain, eliminate sugar from your home and all sources and quantities from your child's diet. Use whole fruit sparingly and closely monitor quantity.

Carbohydrates

Closely related to sugar is the classification of foods to which sugars belong, called carbohydrates. Carbohydrates are commonly considered a fuel source because they become glucose, or blood sugar, upon ingestion.

Carbohydrates include both starches, such as potatoes and breads, and simple sugars, such as those found in white sugar or fruit. Each type of carbohydrate has a glycemic index indicating how fast it will raise glucose levels in the bloodstream (*Sugar Busters!* pg. 44). Some carbohydrates, such as white bread, actually have a higher glycemic index than white sugar, indicating that white bread will actually raise an individual's blood sugar faster than white sugar. Thus, a carbohydrate such as breakfast cereal may actually elevate blood sugar levels faster than a simple sugar does. I have noticed a delicate balance between carbohydrate intake and noticeable reactions in Raja.

Regulating an appropriate carbohydrate intake has been a process of experimentation and close observation. With too many carbohydrates, Raja has visible signs of reaction, including dilated pupils, hyperactivity, and tic-like behavior. Additionally, he clenches his fists, walks on his toes, and opens his mouth wide, holding the position for several seconds. His behavior becomes noticeably autistic and antisocial, preferring to observe moving or spinning objects at close range. He becomes hot to the touch and drinks considerable water. His sleep is fitful, frequently waking, or tossing, turning, and kicking, preferring to keep pressure on the bottom of his feet. Too many carbohydrates—even casein-free, gluten-free carbohydrates—induce joint stiffness and pain, including an emotional edginess perhaps resulting from physical discomfort.

Moreover, many types of carbohydrates appear to induce cravings for further carbohydrates while others do not. While rice does not seem to induce cravings, we do not eat potatoes because potatoes induce cravings for starchy foods. After eating potatoes, cravings for foods such as chips, donuts, popcorn, candy, cookies, pastries, and bread intensify, lasting four days.

Finally, I have observed a progressive build-up of carbohydrates over the course of the day such that an additional intake will cause a reaction. For instance, if the first carbohydrate intake is small, say ¼ of an apple, there will be no reaction. If the second carbohydrate intake is small, say ½ scoop of rice, there will be no reaction. However if either of the above portions were larger, or if a third serving of carbohydrates was ingested, a noticeable reaction would occur.

The connection between carbohydrates and autism should not be overlooked or minimized. While it is important to choose carbohydrates that are well tolerated and do not produce reactions, it is equally critical to monitor your child's carbohydrate intake and find an acceptable balance. An acceptable balance is one that provides energy for fueling reasonable activities while maintaining homeostasis.

For more information regarding carbohydrates and the glycemic index, reference Rick Mendosa's Internet site at www.mendosa.com/gilists.htm.

Chicken Skin and Language Development

Although there is much commotion in medical circles about the role fat plays in the formation of cholesterol and the role cholesterol plays in heart disease, I have noticed a beneficial relationship between Raja's language development and eating cooked chicken skin. Once I noticed a pattern between Raja's language increase and chicken skin, I made a commitment to serve him cooked chicken skin every day. Since then, his language has increased dramatically and there is not as much undigested food in his stools. I believe that chicken skin may contain a digestive enzyme that allows Raja to digest his food more completely, yielding higher quantities of nutrients that support recovery and developmental gain.

Salt

In an attempt to find a type of salt that does not produce a reaction, we have tried sea salt, iodized salt, non-iodized salt, gourmet salt, and rock salt. The only type of salt that Raja can tolerate without a reaction is rock salt. We place rock salt in a salt grinder and grind directly onto food.

"Pure" Ground Beef

Recently, we purchased packages of ground beef that disclosed no ingredient other than ground beef. Reading the labels, the ground beef appeared to be pure, listing only "ground beef" as the ingredient. When consumed, however, the ground beef caused reactions.

Interestingly, the beef was purchased from two different super market chains on separate occasions several months apart. Since the supermarkets are located in the same region, we suspect they purchase their ground beef from the same wholesaler. While the purchasing agents representing the super markets deny purchasing and repackaging impure beef, we suspect that the wholesaler is cutting the beef with an undisclosed ingredient unbeknownst to the super markets. This would explain why the purchasing agents believe they are buying pure ground beef from the wholesaler, yet the "pure" repackaged ground beef caused reactions.

Obviously, this has been very upsetting for us as we work very diligently to be certain Raja's diet is pure. Additionally, every reaction is a costly four-day setback for developmental gain that cannot be recovered. We read labels and cook from scratch specifically to avoid such costly setbacks. Discovering impure beef through reactions is a tragic learning experience in the necessity for homemade ground meat products.

Unfortunately, since we religiously read labels and have found that they cannot always be trusted, it is advisable to purchase only whole meats, fish, and fowl, or to purchase ground meat from a source like Whole Foods Market, where the meat is range fed and store ground using whole products. Additionally, you may consider purchasing and using a meat grinder to be truly safe.

Stick to the List

The list that follows is a compilation of foods and ingredients that must be avoided to maximize recovery and developmental gain. You may wish to photocopy it and keep it in a conspicuous place, such as on the refrigerator door or in your purse or wallet for reference when shopping. I faithfully abide by this list without the slightest deviation.

Quick Reference Sheet For Food and Ingredients to Avoid

Casein. Casein is the protein in milk and is found in all dairy products, mock dairy products made with soy or rice, many health food products, and some canned, frozen, or pre-packaged goods. Dairy products, mock dairy products, and products made with ingredients containing casein must be avoided.

Gluten. Gluten is the protein in wheat, oats, barley, rye, triticale, einkorn, semolina, bulgar, kamut, durum, and spelt. Gluten is also available as a stand-alone product, usually found in health food stores, used to make meat substitutes. Products containing the grains listed above, gluten, or gluten derivatives must be avoided.

Gluten derivatives. Because products containing gluten or gluten derivatives get tricky, a list appears below. Some of these items are processed with flour to prevent sticking or are derived from grains and contain hidden gluten.

Grain vinegar	Grain starches	Grain alcohol	Cinnamon
Vegetable broth	Prepared meats	Curry powder	Mustard
Soy sauce	Horseradish	Malt	Malt syrup
Dextrin	Maltodextrin	Flavorings	Raisins
Dates	Ketchup	Dips	Bacon
Sausage	Hot dogs	Lunch meat	
Modified food starch		Hydrolyzed vegetable protein	
Hydrolyzed plant protein		Textured vegetable protein	

Additives and preservatives. Unfortunately, this list is short compared to the long list of additives and preservatives on the market. The most prudent course of action is to avoid any food or personal care products that contains any item appearing on this list or that you do not otherwise recognize as a natural ingredient.

BHA	BHT	Caseinates
Caffeine	FD&C colors	Calcium Disodium EDTA
MSG	Glutamates	Polysorbate 60, 80
Olestra	Nitrites	Nitrates

Sulfites	Sulfates	Phosphoric acid
Potassium bromate	Metasulfites	TBHQ
Quinine	Vanillin	All aluminum compounds
Nutrasweet	Aspartaime	Annatto color
Natural flavoings	Artificial flavorings	Food coloring

Additives in supplements. This list is certainly short compared to the list of ingredients on most labels. When in doubt, avoid the product or call the manufacturer. A product is not necessarily trustworthy because it was obtained at a health food store (the shelves are lined with forbidden foods and ingredients).

Propylene glycol	Sodium laurel sulfate
Dyes and coloring	Sodium laureth sulfate
Sodium benzoate	Tartrazine
Tocopherol	Magnesium stearate
BHT	BHA

Corn and corn derivatives. Corn is a powerful allergen. Avoid corn, corn derivatives, and products made with corn or corn derivatives.

Corn	Popcorn	Corn syrup
Corn starch	Corn meal	High fructose corn syrup

Sugar. Sugar is responsible for several reactions in Raja, including tactile defensiveness, hyperactivity, dilated eyes, mental stupor, inability to attend and execute instructions, learning disorders, and lack of necessary physical sensation. Scientifically, sugar is represented by words ending in "ose" such as lactose or fructose. Avoid all forms of sugar and any ingredient ending in "ose."

White sugar	Raw sugar	Brown sugar
Turbinado sugar	Maple sugar	Molasses
Corn syrup	Glycerin	Juice (store bought or homemade)
Honey	Fructose	Syrup

Spices. Some spices contain gluten and others produce reactions for reasons not yet understood. This is a list of the spices we have encountered that have caused reactions. Avoid these spices, products containing these spices, and spice mixes containing these spices, such as pumpkin pie spice mix or apple pie spice mix.

Curry powder	Cinnamon	Peppermint
Vanilla	Cloves	Fennel seed
White pepper	Black pepper	Chile pepper
Jalapeno pepper	Allspice	Paprika

Hydrogenated and partially hydrogenated oils. These oils clog the liver—the organ responsible for cleansing the brain. Avoid products with hydrogenated and partially hydrogenated oils.

Living organisms. Yeast and xanthum gum are living organisms that are used in bread and gluten-free products for volume. For maximum developmental gain, avoid foods containing living organisms.

Reviewing this list can be an overwhelming experience. If you are feeling overwhelmed, please know that this feeling is natural and will be alleviated once you have mastered the learning curve associated with implementing Comprehensive Organic Intervention. Mastering the learning curve took about six weeks for me.

One of the ways you might make this transition easier is to join a support group for parents of autistic children (if you do not already belong to one) and begin this program together. With a mutual support system this process may become easier, given opportunities to swap food and recipes. Whether through support or sheer tenacity you will overcome the learning curve if you stay the course. Please stay on track. Without implementing this system you may never know your child as the charming, intelligent, fun-loving person he already is until he is free of autism's distortions.

Step Six:
Food Choices and Preparation

The simplest way to describe food choices and preparation is to say that, except for a few prepared ingredients that may be purchased at the supermarket, all food is purchased whole and made from scratch. I cook from scratch because it is the easiest way to ensure that ingredients are pure. Pure ingredients have the greatest chances of being well tolerated. Additionally, although the term "cooking from scratch" inevitably conjures up images of Grandma bent over the stove hour after hour, cooking from scratch actually streamlined my time.

In the early stages of Comprehensive Organic Intervention, I pored over food labels only to find that many foods did not conform to our dietary guidelines anyway. I found myself devoting an inordinate amount of time to reading labels on cans and boxes and comparing them to a list of prohibited ingredients I kept in my purse. I maintained this routine for months while Raja sat in the shopping cart getting bored and antsy, only to find that a product could not be used because the last few ingredients listed as "spices" or "natural flavorings" were too broad to risk their use. I could have purchased the product, brought it home, contacted the manufacturer, and determined the specifics, but I found this too time and energy consuming. Moreover, food manufacturers often change ingredients without notification, requiring constant verification to avoid potential reactions. Cooking from scratch saves me the hassle of constantly verifying manufacturers' ingredients. More importantly, it saves Raja the developmental loss associated with food-induced reactions.

What We Eat

The following list of foods was compiled by literally opening every kitchen cupboard, the refrigerator, and the freezer, to be certain I did not overlook or assume anything. We eat the foods and use the products that are listed here because they have been tested by us and do not cause reactions in our family. I have listed brand names in cases where we have tried others but encountered reactions. You may wish to photocopy this list and use it for a shopping guide when entering a supermarket or health food store.

Although we do our cooking from scratch, busy people will enjoy the simplicity of this lifestyle because grocery shopping is quick and easy, freeing up time for other activities. I spend my time in two sections of the supermarket—meat and produce—then retrieve specific items from other sections of the store. Because I have memorized the location of the other products we need, I can be in and out of the store in 20 minutes or less, making an occasional trip to the health food store, if necessary. The simplicity of this diet is a real time saver—something I especially appreciate with Raja in tow!

Meat, fish, and poultry: As much as possible, we use whole, range-fed, antibiotic- and hormone-free choices. Read labels carefully and ask questions! We have found the highest quality of meat is usually available at meat markets or health food stores.

Eggs: To the extent possible, we buy eggs from free-roaming chickens that do not receive antibiotics or hormones. Although these eggs are expensive (over $2.00 per carton), they are available at most supermarkets and health food stores.

Peanut and other nut butters: Nut butters must be all natural, free of salt, sugar, partially hydrogenated oils, and preservatives. I have found unsalted, all natural peanut butter at most supermarkets in both crunchy and creamy varieties. Oil separation occurs in all nut butters and is normal. After opening the jar, either stir the oil in, or drain off, as you prefer. Refrigerate after opening.

Vegetables and fruits: To the extent possible, we buy organic produce, which is certified free of pesticides. Many supermarkets carry organic produce and health food stores normally carry a wide selection of organic choices. If you cannot buy organic produce, wash chemically treated produce thoroughly and peel whenever possible.

Herbs and spices: As I mentioned already, the only type of salt we use is rock salt that we pour into a salt grinder and grind directly onto food. Regarding herbs and other spices, the greatest success we have had in avoiding reactions comes from buying whole spices and placing them in spice grinders purchased separately at department stores. Many supermarkets carry whole spices and some whole, inexpensive spices may be found in the Mexican food section. Still, we have had unexpected reactions to some whole seasoning blends, such as Italian seasoning mix, but can use others with success, like the delicious Herbs de Provence. As always, it will be necessary to document the spices you are using and eliminate any that cause a reaction.

The list below includes whole herbs and spices we use without reaction.

Oregano	Herbs de Provence	Bouquet Garni	Cumin
Bay leaves	Basil	Cardamon	Anise
Thyme	Mustard seed	Summer savory	Nutmeg
Pizza seasoning			

Vinegar: Rice vinegar. There are often several types of rice vinegar available in the Asian section of a large supermarket. Be certain the only ingredients are rice and water. Remember that other vinegar, normally found in the condiment section of the supermarket, is made with grain and must be avoided. Although rice is also a grain it is not usually an allergen in our culture. We have experienced no reactions using rice and rice products.

Oil: We use 100% pure olive or canola oil. I have never noticed a reaction to any brand of either of these oils.

Nuts: We buy only whole, unsalted peanuts in the shell, or whole, raw, unsalted, shelled almonds or other nuts. Nuts make a great snack, given that your child has no reactions to them.

Beans: We eat all types of beans except soybeans. We do not eat soybeans because I have read that most of the soybeans produced in the United States have been genetically modified, increasing their chances of inducing a reaction. Presently, genetically modified food does not have to be labeled as such. However, we eat all other types of beans, peas, and lentils, and have never experienced a reaction, whether obtained from bulk bins or pre-packaged. If you buy pre-packaged beans, they must be whole and uncooked and the only ingredient must be beans. Most packages have printed cooking instructions on the back and many include recipes for favorite dishes such as split pea soup. Beans are inexpensive, can be dressed up to be very tasty, can cook by themselves in a crock pot, are a source of protein and fiber, and tend to stretch other food a long way.

Rice: Whether white or brown, rice must be the only ingredient listed on the package or bulk bin from which it is obtained. Do not purchase enriched rice. If rice or other products are obtained from a bulk bin with a scoop, be certain that there are no opportunities for cross-contamination with products containing gluten. It is possible that the customer before you used the rice scoop in the wheat flour, then put the scoop back in the rice bin. Unless the bulk bins are top-loaded and do not require scoops, it may be safer to purchase rice that is pre-packaged, containing only rice. We find plain rice in the Asian section of the supermarket. Additionally, most brown rice is not enriched, making it a good choice, too.

Cereal: The only cereal we have found that does not cause a reaction is Barbara's Brown Rice Crisps. These are very much akin to Rice Krispies in terms of taste, texture, and crackle. Although there are other gluten-fee, rice-based breakfast cereals available at health food stores and supermarkets, this is the only one we have tried that did not cause a reaction. When ground, this cereal makes a nice binder in meat loaf and is adaptable to other foods as well.

Baking and Quick-Bread Products

When baking, always choose gluten-free baking products. Gluten-free products can be located at a health food store, cooperative, or online. A brief list of flours is provided below.

Garbanzo bean flour (yes, I am serious). The batter will taste terrible, like you put beans in it, but the baked product is rich and delicious. This is one of my favorite flours.

White rice flour. Can be a bit grainy when used alone, but when mixed with the right proportion of potato starch flour and tapioca flour, is a close second to wheat flour.

Sweet rice flour. An excellent thickening agent in place of corn starch. Sweet rice flour is also useful in homemade deodorant.

Tapioca flour. Very fine, powdery flour with a silky texture. Fun to run through your hands, just because the texture is so smooth. One of the components in mock wheat flour.

Potato starch flour. Actually smells like potatoes, with a somewhat grainy texture, and I have never used it for anything but making the mock wheat flour.

Baking powder: We use Featherweight Baking Powder, available at health food stores in the baking products section. The label specifies cereal free, gluten-free, sodium free.

Baking soda: We have never had a problem with any brand of baking soda, including store brands available at supermarkets.

Flax seed meal: Flax seed meal has an extremely fishy taste, but is touted to contain Omega-3 fats and has never caused a reaction. Flax seed meal is available at health food stores in the baking goods section.

Carob: Carob is a powder ground from a seed with a flavor akin to cocoa. Use only 100% carob. Avoid products such as carob chips that may contain unacceptable ingredients. Carob is available in health food stores in the bulk foods section.

Egg Replacer: Egg Replacer is a brand-name product and is intended as a substitute for eggs in recipes that call for them. Since refining our diet, I have not had occasion to use Egg Replacer but had previously found that it did not cause a reaction. Egg Replacer comes in a box that is located in the health food store alongside other baking products. The box itself has many recipes printed on it, some of which may be amended for use.

Supplements: Raja receives daily calcium supplementation through Country Life Nerve and Osteo Support. I use half the adult dosage and crush it in a pill crusher (available for under $5 in the pharmacy section at Wal-Mart). The tablets crush up nicely, do not have a noticeable flavor, and can be mixed with anything Raja likes to eat. Look for acceptable supplements at a health food store.

It is worth noting that many whole, frozen products do not contain preservatives and may provide an alternative to keeping only fresh ingredients on hand. Freezing preserves products without preservatives. If you are interested in poring through the frozen food section for acceptable foods, you may find gluten-free bread, fruit, and vegetables. Early in the implementation of this diet, I was so happy to see a pancake mix marked "gluten free" that I excitedly purchased it and used it without reading the label. Of course, Raja had a reaction. I then read the label and found ingredients other than gluten that disqualified the product from use. This was learning the hard way but I only had to learn the lesson once. If you decide to purchase pre-made products in the health food store or supermarket, always read labels and remember that products could have been processed with ingredients likely to cause a reaction.

Foods We Do Not Eat Anymore

Dietary refinements resulting in greater health have eliminated some of the ingredients we used to eat but do not eat anymore. I offer the following list because it may benefit your child. Two of the three ingredients outlined below did not produce a reaction but we avoid them for the health reasons described. Reactions have occurred with the third ingredient, as noted in the text.

Yeast: Since refining the diet, we have not consumed any bread or any products containing yeast, so yeast has presumably disappeared from our digestive tracts. Yeast is associated with Candida, or yeast overgrowth, leading to yeast infections. In the introduction of his book, *Yeast Control In Seven Days*, Dr. Sal D'Onofrio also indicates that yeast is associated with "…digestive problems, blood sugar imbalances, parasites, and concurrent allergies associated with candidiasis" (pg. 1). Yeast is a living organism and it may be prudent to avoid it for the aforementioned reasons.

Xanthum gum: You may have noticed xanthum gum on the label of many prepared foods on supermarket shelves. Like yeast, xanthum gum is a living organism that is used as a binder to give volume to gluten-free foods. We have used xanthum gum sparingly since refining our diet. It may be worth avoiding since it may interrupt natural processes. It is a fairly common ingredient in gluten-free recipes. For maximum developmental gain, avoid use and ingestion.

Flavorings: Flavorings are common in baked goods. The flavorings commonly stocked in supermarkets are made with alcohol—a product that contains gluten and must be avoided. However, Frontier Flavorings makes a line of flavorings that do not contain gluten and may be obtained at the health food store in the baking products or spice section. Unfortunately, we have noticed reactions to all the Frontier Flavorings we tried which may be due to the glycerin used in place of alcohol. (Glycerin is not derived from gluten, but we have found it contains enough sugar to elicit a reaction). Some of their flavorings do not contain glycerin, using canola oil instead, but we have noticed reactions even using these. Your results may vary.

Cooking Methods We Avoid: Although grilled food is very delicious, we have experienced reactions with food that has been grilled, smoked, or barbecued, with or without acceptable sauces or marinades. Thus, we avoid grilled, smoked, or barbecued food.

We have covered all aspects of dietary intervention and will now explore environmental intervention.

Step Seven:
Environmental Intervention

Like dietary intervention, environmental intervention creates opportunities for developmental gain by avoiding contact with substances that create reactions. The purpose of environmental intervention is to maintain a stable state by identifying and removing substances that impair recovery through reactions. Environmental intervention is possible when your child has achieved and maintained a stable state using dietary intervention because a stable state creates a baseline for observing influences that negatively impact recovery. Moreover, symptoms of an environmentally induced reaction may be similar to those experienced with dietary reactions. Thus, Raja's symptoms of reaction include hyperactivity, dilated pupils, and temporary language deficit whether the source of reaction is dietary or environmental. Preventing the interruption of a stable state is the goal of environmental intervention.

Becoming an Environmental Detective

At the height of his autism, Raja would run away when he was not receiving attention so I was constantly assessing and altering his environment to keep him safe. I placed interior locks on the outside door to keep him inside the house when I was out of eyesight. I chained the gate leading to the driveway so he would not run out of the yard if

I turned my head. I always secured him in a shopping cart or firmly held his hand when we were near a street as he had no healthy fear of cars. In many ways, your child has probably already trained you to be an environmental detective. You may already eliminate social events your child would find too challenging or keep an ear posted for the moment a loud noise will send him into shrieks of terror. We have graduated from autism's boot camp. Environmental intervention is a natural outgrowth of the measures you already take to keep your child away from situations he finds socially and behaviorally overwhelming. Environmental intervention extends the kind of evaluations you perform to include the identification and removal of substances that cause reactions.

Environmental substances that cause reactions are usually contacted through touch or inhalation. These substances can be as common as lotion, shampoo, soap, bubble bath, toothpaste, fertilizers, and pesticides. While many of these products contain gluten derivatives and must be avoided for reasons already stated, all of them contain chemicals that may cause reactions. Any product containing chemicals has the potential to induce reactions. Any product that induces a reaction must be identified and eliminated immediately.

Detecting and Eliminating Environmental Hazards

Environmental intervention rests on the same principle as dietary intervention: when contact with substances producing an immune response are avoided, homeostasis is maintained, paving the path for wellness and developmental gain. The purpose of environmental intervention, then, is to identify and eliminate sources of reaction in your child's environments, including home and school and wherever else he spends his time.

When your child exhibits symptoms of reaction, the task at hand becomes detecting and eliminating the triggers. Detecting and eliminating environmental hazards is the second step in securing your child's developmental gain.

Environmental Hazards At Home

The substitutions presented in this chapter range from cooking utensils to toothpaste and require the elimination of any substance that could produce a reaction. A good rule of thumb is to use only products whose ingredients are derived from natural sources.

We do not have pets, but pets and grooming supplies should be a big consideration for your child. Everything from flea and tick powder to dog shampoos and horse sprays may negatively impact your child; caution is the watchword. It is better to be cautious than sorry. Thus, although this list is designed to be comprehensive, it is based on our familial experiences and is intended to act as a springboard for other situations your child may encounter where similar guidelines apply.

Consider the impact of your child's environment on his immune system at all times. Eliminate anything you may suspect that has the potential to cause a reaction. The level of caution you use in determining environmental hazards and your willingness to avoid these hazards will dramatically improve your child's ability to avoid reactions and achieve developmental gain.

Practical Considerations and Social Ramifications

There are two facets of Comprehensive Organic Intervention: the practical considerations and the social ramifications. Obviously, the practical considerations are easier to address, making it easier to replace your pots and pans than to begin cooking with them. While this book largely addresses the practical concerns, it is equally important to consider the social ramifications, including the ability to successfully implement and use this program.

The most important consideration in making successful dietary and environmental transitions is to determine ahead of time that you will stick with it. Our success is dependent on my determination to achieve and maintain a new standard and that, no matter the protests, we are not going back. It has never taken longer than a week (a long week, but a week) for Raja to really understand that we are breaking an old habit. Patiently explaining (often numerous times a day) that we no longer use a product eventually conveys the message. Your consistency and utter reliability will make all the difference in getting your child's cooperation. Understand that your child is breaking a habit and possibly ending an addition. Breaking habits and ending addictions require time and support. You know your child will test you. Be certain that you can remain consistent without taking a step backward.

As a consolation, many substitutions will not impact your child directly, eliminating the power-struggles over relinquishing favorites. However, it was still a transition for *me* to give up *my* favorites, using substitutions for several months before feeling comfortable. Fortunately, the substitutions have delivered the same level of quality I had come to assume previously. While it may be unusual to apply deodorant you have just mixed in the kitchen, rest assured that both Larry and I have tried the alternatives for nine months and would still be looking if the substitutions did not work.

Keeping a lighthearted attitude of experimentation helped me overcome my stubborn tendencies toward habit. Additionally, I was consoled by the knowledge that I was not just helping myself by employing healthy substitutions. Someday Raja will need personal care products like acceptable deodorant and shaving cream. Every courageous step Larry and I take as Raja's partners and role models allows us to gain experiential knowledge that will benefit him in the years to come.

The following environmental considerations represent the processes and replacements we have undertaken to promote Raja's wellness and developmental gain. As you read through the lists, please remember that we did not accomplish this overnight. Since implementing this lifestyle is a large task, I have endeavored to simplify it as much as possible. *It is more important to be consistent in making progress than to implement the whole program at once and get so overwhelmed that it cannot be naturally integrated into your daily routine.* Change is difficult and this is a big and important undertaking. Keep the vision and steadily work toward your goal. You are succeeding as long as you are consistently upholding the present standard and incorporating further change as possible. There is no "right" way to incorporate these changes. The only "wrong" way to implement this program is to give up. Be kind and patient with yourself and your child. Very soon your changes will become habitual.

Organizing the Changes

The tasks have been separated into two categories: processes and replacements. To simplify things, you will find one reference sheet for each of these categories at the end of the chapter. These reference sheets are suitable for reproduction and may be placed in a conspicuous place in the home or given to others whose cooperation is required for your child's benefit (e.g., child care providers, schools, or grandparents).

Two resources are largely responsible for the processes and replacements outlined here: Dr. Hulda Clark's book, *The Cure For All Diseases*, covering everything from parasites to mercury-free dentistry, and *www.thensome.com/cleaning.htm*, a web site for chemically-free living. If you are interested in furthering your study of natural living, you may find these resources helpful.

Quick Reference Guide: Processes

The following processes are steps we take to insure as little contact as possible with environmental substances that could cause a reaction.

1. *Wash eggs.* I have read that the salmonella in eggs is actually on the shells and that washing them thoroughly removes the salmonella. Remove eggs from carton, replace carton in

refrigerator, wash eggs, wash hands, break eggs. This is the process we use.

2. *Never eat food that has fallen on the floor.* Some adults and most children will eat food that has fallen on the floor. Despite floors that may look "clean enough to eat on," floors get constant foot traffic, bringing in dirt, dust, and microscopic organisms. Never eat food that has fallen on the floor.

3. *Never use silverware that has fallen on the floor.* For the same reasons as those stated above, place silverware that falls on the floor in the sink and retrieve a fresh piece before using.

4. *Never let pets eat from plates.* Many pet owners share their table scraps with pets directly from their plates and bowls. Animals have parasites that travel in saliva and can enter and live in human bodies. Contact with pet saliva can transfer unwanted parasites. Place table scraps in pet's bowl. Never share plates or bowls with pets.

5. *Filter water.* Use a water filter that removes as many chemicals as possible. We use a PUR water filter that attaches directly to the faucet and filters up to 40 gallons before needing cartridge replacement. PUR and other water filters are available at department stores.

6. *Add hydrogen peroxide to bath water.* Adding hydrogen peroxide to bath water removes the negative effects of chlorine from entering the system while bathing. Use 2 cups per bath.

7. *Wash all clothes in hot water.* Hot water kills germs. Wash all clothes, bedding, linens, etc. in hot water (as hot as possible).

8. *Wash socks and underwear separately.* Socks and underwear have contact with specific parts of the body. Wash separately in hot water.

9. *Wash all linens that contact food separately.* Linens that contact food, such as kitchen towels, dish rags, napkins, and place mats,

should be washed in hot water separately from other linens and clothing.

10. *Wash hands frequently.* Hands are one of the best ways for germs to travel and spread communicable diseases. When washing, be certain to wash in between the fingers (in the web of the hands). Germs remain in the web of the hands if we only wash the fronts and backs.

11. *Avoid air fresheners, disinfectants, and products with fumes or odors.* Many people are sensitive to airborne particles. Airborne particles can cause reactions.

12. *Avoid insecticides, pesticides, paint, sealants, and other chemical applications.* For the reasons stated above, avoid products containing chemicals, including those applied directly to skin such as insect repellents.

13. *Avoid personal care products containing or expelling chemicals.* Avoid hair sprays, mousse, gels, coloring, shaving cream, deodorant, shampoo, conditioner, bath bubbles, bath gels, body wash, etc. that contain or expel (from a propellant container) products containing chemicals. Even residues can cause reactions.

14. *Avoid most makeup.* Most makeup contains chemicals that will cause a reaction even if hypoallergenic or procured from a company that does not do animal testing. Mothers must avoid wearing lipstick as it may contact a child's skin and cause a reaction from a kiss on the lips or cheek. Avoid direct application of makeup for dress up, Halloween, or school plays.

15. *Avoid mercury dental fillings.* Mercury is the second deadliest substance known to man (plutonium is the first), and can cause cognitive and nervous system disorders. It leaches from teeth into the bloodstream, causing immune responses and degenerative disorders. Biological Dentistry offers an alternative. Biological Dentists test an individual's blood for

reactive agents and find several alloys that are compatible with blood factors. You will find a resource for Biological Dentists on the Internet by entering Biological Dentists in the search engine. Additionally, you may find a Biological Dentist in the phone book or consult an herbalist, Doctor of Naturopathy, or Doctor of Oriental Medicine for a referral to a Biological Dentist in your area.

Quick Reference Guide: Replacements

1. *Pots, pans, and bakeware*: We have replaced all cookware with non-toxic alternatives consisting of glass, cast iron, or ceramic. I have read time and again that the aluminum in aluminum cookware enters food through contact and can be absorbed while eating. Aluminum is believed to be one of the metals responsible for Alzheimer's disease. To avoid unnecessary contamination, switch to glass, cast iron, or ceramic cookware, which can be purchased at most department stores. Read all manufacturer's suggestions before use.

2. *Dish washing detergent, laundry detergent, hand soap, and general home cleaning*: We use 20 Mule Team Borax. 20 Mule Team Borax is a brand-name product that serves many purposes, including washing our dishes, whether by hand or in the dishwasher. Dish washing soaps and liquids leave a film on dishes that may adhere to foods and inadvertently be consumed while eating. Although 20 Mule Team Borax may do the same, it is a natural product and contains antiseptic qualities, so its inadvertent consumption is not as harmful. However, it makes no suds and feels slightly gritty on the hands. I find it most convenient to leave a small dish full near the sink and dip into it as necessary for rinsing hands, eggs, or dishes. In the dishwasher, I pour it in the built-in containers like one would with any dish washing detergent. In the laundry, I pour it over the loaded

clothes before I turn the water on. It is a good cleaning agent and can be used for toilet bowls, mopping, cleaning bathtubs and sinks, and removing grease from the stove. 20 Mule Team Borax is available in many supermarkets in the laundry detergent section near the laundry boosters.

3.   *Eliminate fabric softeners and dryer sheets*: We do not use fabric softeners or dryer sheets.

4.   *Toothpaste*: We use baking soda. Baking soda is a non-toxic, inexpensive alternative that has not caused a reaction with any brand we have tested. It is also an effective cleaning and whitening agent for household use.

5.   *Deodorant:* We use a homemade recipe consisting of 50% vitamin C powder and 50% sweet rice flour that is placed in a large, plastic shaker for convenient application. Vitamin C powder kills bacteria and sweet rice flour is a non-reactive agent used to bind the vitamin C powder to the skin. Both products are available at a health food store.

6.   *Soap and shampoo*: We use 100% glycerin soap, unscented and without coloring. You may have seen this transparent soap before as it is widely available at most supermarkets. 100% glycerin soap may be found in either the soap section or with the cosmetics. Used as shampoo, it will not lather as other shampoos, but cleans just as well.

7.   *Shaving cream*: 100% glycerin soap, unscented and without coloring.

8.   *Hair conditioner:* We use pure aloe vera juice. We buy a large jug, available at the supermarket or department store, and pour it in a small container kept in the shower. You may know aloe vera for its healing qualities on cuts and scrapes. It also appears to stop the flaking and itching associated with dandruff and leaves hair very soft and manageable. (Surprisingly, it is even easy to comb hair while wet, which is a wonderful plus for kids). Again,

like most of these replacement products, it is different from other hair conditioners, but works extremely well and does not produce a reaction.

9. *Skin lotion and lip moisturizer:* We use a 50% solution of pure aloe vera juice and canola oil that we mix well and keep in containers for use. You may also wish to contact Special Foods! and review the list of products they offer. Special Foods! specializes in hypoallergenic foods and personal care products. Special Foods! may be reached at (703) 644-0991 or 9207 Shotgun Court, Springfield, VA 22153. You may also wish to request the handout they produce for parents of autistic children.

10. *Cosmetics:* I have been only moderately successful finding recipes for natural cosmetics. While I have not found a lipstick replacement that I like, I have switched my eye liner to artist's charcoal (available in an art or hobby supply store in the art section) with success. Since skin is porous, cosmetics are absorbed by the skin and can cause a reaction. Charcoal, on the other hand, is a natural product and can be absorbed by the skin without reaction. If you are looking for lipstick or foundation replacements, it may be worth investigating at the library or on the Internet. I believe mascara is acceptable, provided it only contacts the eyelashes and not the skin.

11. *Contact solution:* We use over-the-counter solutions. However, there are recipes available for making contact solutions at home in Dr. Hulda Clark's book, *The Cure For All Diseases.*

12. *Wear cotton clothing (Raja):* Raja has a reaction to clothing made of synthetic products so we place cotton clothing next to his skin. In other words, if Raja sleeps in pajamas made of polyester (most pajamas are made with polyester), he wears cotton underclothes next to his skin and his pajamas layered on top.

This concludes the processes and replacements that foster developmental gain by avoiding substances that may cause reactions. However, I would like to leave you with a rule I apply when in doubt.

The Rule

In promoting environmental wellness, it is wise to err on the side of caution. If a product has a label, read it. Before using a product, investigate the ingredients by calling the manufacturer or contacting him online. Avoid anything containing chemicals, including bubble bath, body wash, perms, hair coloring, cleaning agents, and car wax. Avoid anything that is scented, including perfume, cleaning agents, carpet fresheners, plug-in air fresheners, and potpourri. Watch for a reaction to flowers (some people are unfortunately allergic to flowers). Avoid anything that leaves a residue in the air due to burning, such as cigarette smoke or incense. Avoid anything that is colored, including finger paints, face or body paints, henna, or other tattoos. Avoid modeling clay, play clays, and slime, unless homemade using acceptable ingredients. Avoid body piercing and permanent tattoos. Closely watch for reactions from jewelry and clothing that contact the skin.

Never permit your child to play in or around an area that has been recently sprayed with pesticides, herbicides, or that may contain residues. Avoid any construction or painting zone and remove your child from your home when these are taking place. Drink and swim in clean, clear water, avoiding chlorine and other chemicals as much as possible. Try to avoid city smog and pollution; breathe fresh air.

If your child is going to spend the night outside of your home, investigate the new environment and eliminate opportunities for reactions. Whether this is grandma's house or the sitter's, all of the environments in which your child spends time must conform to his needs. While you are preventing him from ingesting forbidden food, also investigate and prepare his away-from-home environments, paving the way for his developmental gain.

Discuss your child's dietary and environmental needs with the school principal and teacher and gain their cooperation. Notice and eliminate any smells in the classroom, including perfume. Investigate the content of your child's school supplies (especially paper) and call the manufacturer to confirm content. If necessary, switch paper. Investigate your child's classroom and play areas and work to eliminate opportunities for reactions.

Discuss your child's dietary and environmental needs with his therapists and gain their cooperation in eliminating any therapeutic devices or processes that may provoke a reaction. Remember that many substances used in therapy, such as shaving cream or pudding, may cause a reaction. Work with therapists to supply appropriate substitutes.

We have illuminated the concept and application of environmental intervention. We will now discuss challenging situations and ways to make this lifestyle more practical in everyday circumstances.

Step Eight:
The Lifestyle

Comprehensive Organic Intervention is a lifestyle that promotes recovery and developmental gain based on eliminating food and non-food substances that cause reactions. Since this is a lifestyle, it is important to practice and model it as such since it will likely be your child's way of life forever.

Below you will find ideas pertaining to situations you may encounter that may make living the lifestyle easier. As you will see, many of these suggestions are just creative twists on old themes while others will offer some options for situations you may encounter. Since food is a common theme in most celebrations, food issues are addressed here and substitutions offered. If your family is highly traditional, consider this lifestyle a new tradition. Think of ways you can make new rituals by incorporating substitutions in your traditions. It is always helpful to be creative and lighthearted about change. If you find yourself resenting any part of this process, grieve the losses you may feel in giving up traditions or find new and meaningful ways to replace those traditions with your family.

Tradition

Tradition makes us feel good. It is difficult for us to give up traditions because their familiarity imparts a sense of comfort and we want this comfort to be experienced by our children. However, when traditions incorporate harmful food and environmental substances that may provoke reactions, we may be comforted by the knowledge that new traditions can become equally familiar over time. As old traditions are replaced with more appropriate choices, our children are rewarded with new traditions that fully support recovery and developmental gain.

For instance, our old tradition when decorating the Christmas tree was to play Christmas music and drink hot chocolate. This year we roasted chestnuts instead. Warm chestnuts are rich and satisfying. They are also expensive, making them a special treat we will incorporate during tree decoration. For Larry and me, roasting chestnuts represents a new tradition. On the other hand, Raja will grow up roasting chestnuts and will likely repeat this tradition with his family.

One of the easiest ways to make substitutions in traditional rituals is to do advance planning, allowing your child to partake of holidays, but in ways that support his recovery. Since traditions involving food are commonplace during the holidays, you will find suggestions for substitutions below. Additionally, information pertaining to everyday situations is included. I hope these suggestions are helpful.

Holidays

Easter. The biggest Easter issue is replacing the candy in the traditional Easter basket with an acceptable alternative. Obvious substitutions are toys, books, CDs, and educational videos. Consider plastic eggs that can be filled with balls, puzzle pieces, or money. Also, small handmade coupons would fit nicely inside eggs and may be redeemable for things your child would like, such as a movie rental or a trip to a local attraction. Easter baskets do not have to be filled with candy to be fun. Your thoughtfulness and creativity will make any basket fun to receive.

Valentine's Day. Again, the issue here is candy. Replace the candy with alternatives that that your child would appreciate, expressing your love. Toys, books, CD-ROMs, and videos are good choices, but so is a heart-shaped homemade treat that conforms to dietary guidelines. You might take your child on a favorite outing or spend time with him doing a favorite activity. Anything that expresses love that does not produce a reaction is a good alternative for Valentine's Day.

Halloween. Traditionally, Halloween is a candy-fest, but there are alternatives. Giving candy to trick-or-treaters inevitably means keeping candy in the house, so we give away party favors instead. Rather than candy, we have a huge bowl filled with everything from squishy heads to life-like spiders, rats, bats, mummies, witches, and happy-face bubbles for the little ones. The kids love them. The leftovers make great party favors or treats for next Halloween.

Regarding Halloween parties, it may be easiest to throw your own or to take your child to a haunted house instead. Many cities have age-appropriate haunted houses where children can be delighted being spooked or play games that involve prizes. Larry's younger brother, Tom, was highly allergic to candy as a child. He was also the envy of his friends. Instead of trick-or-treating, Tom got to go to all the haunted houses in the city and tell his friends all the details the next day at school. Rather than being the misfit, Tom was the post-Halloween king for a day, recounting gory details to a host of delighted peers who hung on his every word.

I think we are often mistaken when we believe that our children will be missing out on something if they are unable to do what we did, or eat what we ate, as kids. I also think that, in our culture, we sometimes offer candy and treats instead of spending quality time together, using a sweet incentive to endear someone, especially a child, rather than developing a relationship. Candy and treats are a shortcut to something much deeper that we are actually craving—purity of heart, the soul companionship of another, and the selfless giving that comes of having one's needs taken into consideration and creatively attended.

Rather than Halloween parties filled with sweets where kids end up bouncing off the walls, perhaps we can fill our parties with fun games, such as bobbing for apples, spooky stories told by flashlight or candlelight, or presents and surprises that bring laughter and joy. We can make Halloween decorations, do plays, or have talent contests. Children really seek our company and our devoted attention more than candy. It is not so much what we give them, but how we can attend to them, that is memorable in the end.

Thanksgiving and Christmas. Regarding food, Thanksgiving and Christmas are virtual free-for-alls, where everything from the "naturally flavored" turkey to the pumpkin pie is destined to cause reactions. This is unfortunate, but does not relegate us to holiday outcasts. Instead, we may (or must) bring our own dishes that are appropriate for our families and share ours with others.

This year, our family was fortunate enough to befriend a new family and be invited to their lovely home for Thanksgiving. Instead of declining, we prepared our own meal and brought enough to share. We had meat, sweet potatoes, cranberry sauce, vegetables, salad, candy, and pie. All of it conformed to our diet. We were able to enjoy their company and they sampled our food. It was a wonderful day; bringing our meal worked out well. It presented no hassles for them in trying to accommodate different dietary guidelines and allowed us to eat without worry or question.

Birthdays: The traditional focus of a birthday party is the birthday cake. A lavishly decorated birthday cake takes center stage at the dining room table and people can hardly resist licking the frosting before the cake is cut. The good news is children employing Comprehensive Organic Intervention do not have to go without birthday cake! There is a recipe for a delicious fruit-sweetened birthday cake and frosting in the

Recipe section. One of the bigger differences in creating the lavish decorations atop the cake is that toys or edible flowers must take the place of frosting flowers on traditional birthday cakes.

Everyday Circumstances

We lead busy lives. Because Comprehensive Organic Intervention requires cooking from scratch, preparation is the one activity that will significantly reduce the stress of everyday circumstances. Preparation alleviates the desire to succumb to prepared food, avoiding the reactions that are inevitable with outside food sources. Whether driving around town or taking an extended vacation, preparation makes the journey much more pleasant and relaxing. Prepare foods that your child can eat and keep them handy for snacking. Additionally, many foods that Raja takes in the car do not require actual cooking, so being prepared does not necessarily mean cooking. It only references a process that has made our lives infinitely easier and less stressful.

Other everyday circumstances include interacting with others. Some suggestions follow for meeting challenges in public situations.

Outside the Home

People often offer Raja treats. When a stranger offers to give Raja a treat, I say, "Thank you very much, but Raja is recovering from autism. We can't eat sweets." If you don't feel comfortable telling someone your child is recovering from autism, you do not have to offer explanations. Just politely decline the treat.

When traveling to a family member's home, such as Grandma's house, bring treats that your child can eat and give them to Grandma to offer your child. This way your child can eat a treat and Grandma can feel good about offering something your child can safely consume.

When dining or staying with friends in their home, we bring food we can eat and cook the meals.

If your child might find himself in circumstances where other children are eating things that he cannot have, preparing an equivalent will make things much easier for him. For example, if the other children are having cookies, keeping some cookies or other treats that conform to the diet on hand will ease the transition. Many treats can be kept in the freezer and defrosted when needed. Bring treats to any environment where your child may unexpectedly find himself encountering unacceptable treats. Place acceptable treats in the freezer for future use.

Interestingly, because we eat so little fruit, fruit is just as enticing as treats for Raja. He will gladly eat fruit while the other kids are having their treats because fruit is a treat for him. This has come in handy, especially at others' homes, because most people tend to keep fruit on hand. Raja will gladly eat an apple or pear while the other kids are eating cookies or ice cream and not feel he is being left out.

If your child is done eating his treat but the other children are going back for seconds and you feel your child should not eat more, prepare to engage him in an activity he likes or take him outside, away from the other kids.

Food can be quite addictive and your child may have difficulty in situations where food is being served that he cannot eat. Until the manifestations of food addiction are gone (e.g., having a tantrum if he cannot have a certain food), you may find yourself working very hard to keep him away from food he cannot have. If this is too much work for you, which it was for me, try to avoid situations that may be difficult until you are ready. For Raja, it took about two months to be able to walk away from food he could not have without crying. From two to six months, having alternative food was very important. At six months, the desire to eat forbidden food appeared to be gone. Since then, it has been easy to walk past food that used to elicit tantrums.

Teach your child the meaning of "That's not ours" or "We don't eat that" so he will not eat what is not acceptable. Raja knows and respects "That's not ours." Even when we have eaten with friends in their home and their children have put something on the table that Raja cannot have, he will not try to eat it when he hears, "That's not ours."

Whenever we leave the house, I pack a backpack that has a few snacks and some water in case Raja gets hungry or thirsty while away from home. Common snacks are almonds, cooked chicken or jerky, and peeled, baby carrots.

When we are planning day trips or road trips I cook in advance, preparing foods that one would take on a picnic that are easy to eat and taste good cold. We have plenty of vegetables with dressing, fruit, meatballs (beef, turkey, or chicken), and rice salad. I have prepared marinated chicken breasts and cut the meat into small pieces for snacking or made chicken wings or thighs that Larry and Raja like cold. We pack food and ice in portable coolers and we are ready to go. If we are on a road trip and will be stopping at a hotel overnight, we try to get a room with a microwave, heating the meat once we arrive. This breaks up the monotony of always eating cold food. If we know we will be using overnight accommodations, I can include food that is only good warmed, such as stew or goulash. We then enjoy a hearty dinner.

We have been camping while engaged in this lifestyle and found that it was not difficult to meet our needs. However, we were not backpacking in the wilderness; we were in a campground that was only several miles drive from the nearest natural foods store and meat market. Regarding produce, we purchased in quantities that would last several days. Regarding meat, we purchased only what we could eat for a day or two, keeping it iced in the coolers. While Larry likes leftovers, Raja and I tend to prefer food that is cooked and eaten just after preparation. Purchasing meat frequently worked for us but you may wish to modify the system to suit your family's needs. We camped for two weeks this way and had a glorious time.

We have eaten in restaurants less than ten times and every time Raja has had a reaction. Regardless of the number of questions we asked and how careful we attempted to be (including bringing some food ourselves and asking the cook to warm it up), we have never walked away from a restaurant without a reaction. If you enjoy restaurants as much as I used to this information may present a difficult adjustment. However, I think there may be a way around it. Choose a restaurant that is likely to conform to our dietary specifications and speak with the owner or manager. See if there is any way you can work with them to offer a plate that conforms to dietary guidelines. Most people are very kind and want to help. Make suggestions and get involved in the process. You may be surprised at others' enthusiasm in working with you to create something special that works for you and your family.

We have completed the dietary and environmental changes comprising Comprehensive Organic Intervention. We will now address the cumulative effects of intervention by outlining the changes that have occurred to date, including additional steps taken to augment developmental gain.

Where Are We Now?

Our family is nearing the end of nine months in this lifestyle. Raja now speaks in six-word sentences. He talks to me not just when I speak to him, but to communicate with me as normally developing children do. He is eager to learn everything I can present to him. His demeanor is calm. He engages in imaginary play and likes to pretend. For a long time he has been engaging with other children in physical games, such as chase, but is now learning to engage in games requiring social skills. As we remain faithful to this lifestyle the benefits accumulate and appear to be multiplying.

Additionally, as we progress down this path, Raja's dietary choices appear to be changing without negatively impacting his developmental gain. For example, he is not eating chicken skin as frequently, choosing to eat the meat instead. Moreover, he is eating plain carob in a bowl at least once a day, which also appears to facilitate his language gain. Gauging exactly the right amount of fruit and carbohydrates does not appear to be as critical as it used to be. Raja's reactions are getting fewer and further between. Except when he gets *really* excited, all indications of tic-like behavior are gone. Every day, Raja is recovering his ability to process and function as a normally developing child. The Herculean effort originally required to achieve and maintain homeostasis has diminished considerably.

While Comprehensive Organic Intervention constitutes the bulk of our endeavors to promote Raja's recovery, I would be remiss if I did not mention the other interventions we have employed to facilitate speech and cognitive growth. If any of them seem right for you and your child, I would encourage you to try them and observe the results.

First, after Raja was evaluated developmentally delayed, we began learning sign language—at least the cursory language necessary to communicate certain things to Raja and have him communicate them back. I wanted our family to learn sign language because I believed it would help Raja understand the dynamic flow of communication; that language is not just for receiving messages to him but also for communicating his wants and needs with us. Raja responded very well to sign language. He began learning signs for common things like eat, drink, more, trains, etc. Sign language was extremely helpful, giving us a cursory method of communication. It also provided an adjunct form of communication while Raja was learning to talk.

Second, when we had been employing Comprehensive Organic Intervention for two months, I started raising my level of expectations for Raja. For instance, Raja learned to get dressed and undressed, he was potty trained, and I assertively sought his eye contact when talking to him. He did not like doing these things initially, but with insistence and encouragement, Raja began to try and was proud of his progress.

On the other hand, I had some obstacles to overcome, especially when it came to eye contact. I pointed my first and middle fingers at my eyes, requesting Raja to look at me. If he did not look at me, I would gently move his chin so that he eyes would look at mine. He did not like this and would move his head toward me but avert my eyes. Nonetheless, we continue using this skill to this day and Raja's eye contact becomes more appropriate and natural all the time. Although we have to teach our children many of the skills that normally developing children achieve on their own, Raja is very proud of himself when he achieves new levels of independence.

I did not push Raja to achieve anything that he clearly was not ready to attain. However, I do push him. We spend several hours a day working on developmental gain—not always one-on-one, as much of it occurs with learning games on the computer. We draw and cut letters out of construction paper and paste them on the wall. We take walks and talk about the things we see. We say a word and the letter the word begins with, drawing the letter in the air. We blow bubbles and blow out candles. We kick balls and leaves. We use his alphabet machine and learning videos. We count everything from how many engines are pulling a train to how many cows are in a field. We endeavor to make everyday experiences learning experiences.

However, if Raja is not ready for something, I do not force him into situations that overwhelm him. Overwhelming him will only frustrate us both. Paying close attention to him allows me to gauge whether he is ready to be challenged in a new direction. A protest that he does not want to put his shirt on is not the same as shutting down or having a complete temper tantrum. In Raja's case, a protest indicates that he would prefer not to try but he could be consistently encouraged and make progress. A meltdown indicates I am asking him to do something that is presently beyond his comfort level. It would be best to hold off a while and try again at a later date.

For us, one of the giant steps in encouraging Raja's language occurred after seeing the movie, *Thomas And The Magic Railroad* in a theater. When the movie was over, Raja motioned with his hand that he was blowing the train whistle and made a whistling sound with his mouth. It was the first time he had ever imitated a sound! It was also my first clue regarding a direction for encouraging speech. Our home is now a virtual shrine to Thomas the Tank Engine. Thomas has demonstrated mechanical concepts that Raja understands, such as pushing and pulling, and emotional concepts such as asking "please." If your child has a favorite object or character, it can be an excellent teaching tool. Incorporate it in his daily routine as often as possible to stimulate developmental gain.

Finally, despite his prior inability to reciprocate, I have always known that Raja feels my love for him and I openly express it. Showering Raja with patience and kindness requires excellent self-care and constant reminders regarding keeping my actions in line with my true priorities. Additionally, it requires staying in touch with loving feelings so I can prevent their loss. I find it imperative to be well rested and to create time to do things I find personally rewarding.

While there are still gaps in Raja's communication and his desire to interact with strangers at group gatherings, Raja's recovery has far exceeded my greatest hopes. Although I work toward full recovery, I am totally satisfied at this point. I have never worked so hard nor cried more tears of joy than during the last nine months. Whereas the bleak days of autism seemed to stretch endlessly before us, our moments are now punctuated by delightful surprises: new words, improved eye contact, imagination, cognitive abilities. On Christmas day, Raja began calling me Mama. Perhaps for my birthday, he will say, "I love you."

I am frequently moved by things Raja says that touch my heart. Recently, Larry reminded Raja that it was nearing bedtime. As Raja dashed toward his bedroom, he squealed, "Yippee!" Hearing Raja speak is a dream come true. His words dangle in the air like a chorus of invisible miracles. These are the moments a prayer comes to life in a warm hug and a soft voice telling me to, "Sweepy tight."

Today, I glance over at Raja holding his new Buzz Lightyear action figure, dipping and raising Buzz in the air. Raja tells me, "Buzz flies in space." I watch in amazement as Buzz flies through the living room and kitchen, performing magical feats of daring and courage. Raja takes Buzz through the dining room and down the hall, repeating Buzz's famous line, "To infinity and beyond." If autism has given me one gift, it is the experience of taking nothing for granted. I am mesmerized by a son I once doubted I would know. Every word is a treasured jewel.

Every milestone, a hard won celebration. Like Pinocchio's Geppetto, I dreamed of a real boy; at long last, I have one.

Where Do We Go From Here?

Comprehensive Organic Intervention facilitated nothing short of a miracle: it transformed a terrorized, hypersensitive, anti-social child into a bright and animated boy who is a sheer delight to know and love. While it is my sincere hope that every special needs' parent becomes aware of the efficacy of Comprehensive Organic Intervention, the goal of organizing environments to promote recovery creates its own set of guidelines. As a people and a nation, we must be willing to do what is right by our children. It is time we embraced a healing model for special needs children, realigning the environments that serve them to meet this goal.

Create Comprehensive Organic Classrooms

Young children focus much of their learning on creative endeavors, such as arts, crafts, and making food. It would be wonderful to create classrooms with teachers who practice only Comprehensive Organic Intervention, where the environments and curriculums are safe havens for our vulnerable children. First, it would allow our children a safe environment where they could freely explore anything in the classroom without experiencing a reaction. Second, because this lifestyle will likely be the one our children must always follow, developing cooking skills as early as possible is important as well as enjoyable. Third, having a classroom dedicated to Comprehensive Organic Intervention means children would be learning with peers how to investigate and develop alternatives that work for all of them, not just a special exception in the classroom. This would also ease the burden on parents practicing Comprehensive Organic Intervention, who would otherwise be responsible for supplying the exceptions needed in the classroom. Finally, with a classroom full of children who have the same needs, none of the children will feel that they are "different" or "difficult to accommodate," instead feeling the self-esteem generated by designing math, science, art, and English projects that facilitate learning in an appropriate environment. The significance of developing self-esteem for these children cannot be underestimated. For this reason alone, it would be worth creating Comprehensive Organic Classrooms.

Reject Genetically Modified Food

Genetically modified organisms, or GMOs, refer to foods that have been genetically altered to attain a product that is considered superior to the original. GMOs combine various genetic characteristics from different food sources to create new foods that do not exist in nature and are inherently unnatural in the food chain. GMOs are widely supported by the government and, at the printing of this book, do not have to be labeled as such. GMOs are considered superior products because they are the recipients of several desirable traits from various foods that are combined to yield a specific product. For instance, a GMO may be a potato that does not get brown when peeled and exposed to air, or a soybean crop that is genetically modified to be pest-resistant. While genetically modified food may sound like a high-tech solution, I believe it is an allergic nightmare waiting to fully manifest itself. We have yet to know the vast ramifications GMOs will have on people and nature.

Our children need their food, water, air, and play environments as wholesome and natural as possible. GMOs are the worst possible food choices for them because technologists have taken food to a new extreme, making additives and preservatives look ridiculously antiquated in their application. If our children cannot handle additives and preservatives, imagine what will happen when they routinely encounter foods with multiple genetic combinations that are not even properly labeled for prudent selection! Even seed packets may contain genetically altered seeds, so growing your own garden to alleviate the need for store-bought produce may not be a good option unless the seeds have not been genetically modified.

If you would like more information regarding GMOs, there is a coalition of mothers called The Mothers For Natural Law who want to protect the right to know what our food contains. The Mothers For Natural Law produces a highly informative magazine called "*Safe Food News.*" You may obtain further information or join the organization by calling 1-800-REAL-FOOD.

Joining Forces with Other Special Needs Parents

Gathering with other parents of special needs' children can be an empowering process. Many parents join a group for personal support and encouragement, but many are also willing to get in the ring and fight for our children's rights and health issues. When we gather together we have a voice. We also demonstrate strength in numbers. It can be immensely challenging to use up what little respite time you have to attend a meeting, but without each other we lack understanding, camaraderie, and the ability to initiate social change.

There are national and local chapters of the Autism Society of America, as well as regional groups with a special needs focus. To locate a group near you, check online, the newspaper, regional family newsmagazines (they are often free at grocery or book stores and usually have a list of resources that includes local groups for various types of special needs), the phone book, the library, or a local pediatrician and ask for a referral to a local group serving special needs' families. Many people prefer not to join groups, having experienced them as "clickish" and politicized. However, I urge you to try joining a group because you may be pleasantly surprised. You may find great inspiration and encouragement in the greatest extended family I have ever had the privilege of joining—America's special needs' parents.

Recipes

Although the following recipes conform to Comprehensive Organic Intervention guidelines, I caution you to exercise careful observation of your child as he may react to one or more of the ingredients called for here. Closely observe your child, continue your journal entries, and you will successfully fine-tune foods and ingredients that must be avoided.

Please bear in mind that cooking and baking are more of an art than a science for me; I usually put in the pot whatever seems appropriate at the time (given that everything in our house conforms to dietary guidelines). Thus, all quantities are really just guidelines. Experiment and see what suits your fancy.

I commonly use ripe bananas for adding sweetness to deserts. Bananas are a wonderful sweetener, provided they are very ripe. Bananas that are almost black are ideal, as they are very sweet and easy to mash. I have used bananas that are not fully ripened, but prefer bananas that are soft to the touch and brown/black in color.

Many soups, traditional dishes, and main courses are easily adaptable on this diet. We regularly eat things such as roasted chicken, stew, stir fry, steak, goulash, and meat and onions, which are familiar, comforting foods. Additionally, it is possible to make delicious meat loaf and breakfast scrambles by varying ingredients and spices. Although the number of ingredients may seem limited, the possible combinations are many. Familiarity with ingredients' properties (e.g., sweet rice flour is a thickener like corn starch and can be used in gravies as well as baking) will provide confidence in making a reasonable guess at which combinations will yield what results. Your confidence will also multiply exponentially through experience.

To your child's recovery and developmental gain!

Gluten-free Flour Mixes

The following flour mixes come from the excellent cookbook, The Gluten-free Gourmet Cooks Fast and Healthy *by Bette Hagman. The Light Bean Flour Mix has been amended to suit our guidelines. These mixes are used in various recipes in this section.*

Ms. Hagman has done an outstanding job of blending flours that produce delicious results. Incidentally, the Gluten-free Flour Mix substitutes cup-for-cup for wheat flour. However, the taste and texture will vary from wheat flour. For a detailed description of flours that may be used on this diet and what to expect (not to mention a brief, but well-written account of celiac disease and its manifestations), purchase a copy of The Gluten-free Gourmet Cooks Fast and Healthy. *It is the one cookbook to which I am constantly referring, despite the fact that many of the ingredients have to be amended to suit our purposes. I greatly admire Ms. Hagman's pioneering spirit and endless efforts to create recipes that promote wellness and taste wonderful as well!*

Gluten-free Flour Mix
6 cups rice flour
2 cups potato starch flour (be certain it is potato *starch* flour and not potato flour)
1 cup tapioca flour
Place all ingredients in a large, airtight bowl. Mix well and cover. Store in cupboard or freezer for future use.

Light Bean Flour Mix
3 cups garbanzo bean flour
3 cups sweet rice flour
3 cups tapioca flour
Place all ingredients in a large, airtight bowl. Mix well and cover. Store in cupboard or freezer for future use.

Raja's Birthday Cake

This is a very tasty cake, although it will be much browner than you expect most cakes to be. I have found that sweetening recipes with fruit dramatically increases the baking time due to the increased moisture provided by the fruit. Although the cake will appear very brown while baking, do not remove from the oven until it has pulled away from the sides of the pan and/or a knife inserted in the middle comes out clean. The middle has a tendency to be gooey if the cake does not bake long enough. Although I normally stay away from xanthum gum, I have used it here because it is a binder and because we only eat birthday cake three times a year. Storing the xanthum gum in the freezer appears to give it quite a long shelf life. This recipe was adapted from Special Diets For Special Kids by Lisa Lewis, Ph.D.

2 ½ cups gluten-free flour (recipe in this section)
1 tsp. baking soda
2 tsp. xanthum gum
3 tsp. baking powder
½ tsp. salt
4 eggs
1 cup canola oil
1 2/3 cups very ripe mashed bananas
1 cup apple juice (filtered or unfiltered)

Combine first five ingredients and set aside. With electric mixer, blend eggs, oil, and bananas. Beat so well that oil is completely emulsified and the mixture is light. Turn mixer to low. Add flour mixture and juice. Beat minimally on low speed until blended.

Grease and flour (using gluten-free flour) two round cake pans, or one 9x13 pan. Bake at 350 degrees for 30 minutes. After 30 minutes, remove cakes and cover with aluminum foil to prevent further browning. Continue baking 30 minutes or until done.

Banana Carob Pudding

This easy, delicious pudding is a favorite of ours and can be made very quickly after dinner. Additionally, it has doubled as frosting for Raja's birthday cake. I was even able to pipe "Happy Birthday, Raja", provided the pudding was blended until very smooth. To use this recipe as frosting, simply multiply the ingredients to the desired amount (I multiplied the recipe by four to frost and pipe two 8" cake rounds). Ripe bananas are the trick to sweet pudding. Try altering the spice for a different taste, if desired.

Banana Carob Pudding also makes a lovely, uncooked pie filling. Simply add to a homemade, pre-baked pie crust and refrigerate.

2 bananas, sliced
6 tbsp. carob
3 tbsp. canola oil
¼ tsp. ground anise
1 tbsp. water (omit if thicker pudding desired)

Place all ingredients in a blender. Blend until smooth. Refrigerate if desired. Makes 2 big or 3 regular servings.

Peanut Butter Banana Cookies

These cookies are very easy and tasty. However, peanuts are a common allergen, so watch carefully to see if your child is negatively impacted in any way. Along with recognizable signs of reaction, also watch for problems with digestion or elimination, which are indicators that your child is not tolerating a food well. Eliminate anything that is not well tolerated. .

These cookies do not have a long shelf life, perhaps three days at most. However, it has never been a problem in our house because they are gone before spoilage becomes an issue!

2 bananas
½ cup peanut butter, rounded
1 tbsp. + 1 tsp. carob

Mash bananas in a bowl. Add peanut butter and carob. Mix well. Drop by rounded teaspoonful onto ungreased cookie sheet. Bake at 350 degrees for 7-9 minutes or until the bottom appears brown. Lift carefully from cookie sheet and place on cooling rack until cool to the touch. Makes about one dozen cookies.

You-Can-Do-It Quick Bread

This recipe appeared on a package of a Bob's Flour Mill Tapioca Flour and has been amended to our guidelines. Since it does not contain sugar, it is not a sweet bread. The texture is similar to angel food cake. It is delicious topped with fresh fruit or Banana Carob Pudding. Spices, such as ground nutmeg, may be added to vary flavor.

4 eggs, separated
1 tbsp. apple or orange juice
½ cup Bob's tapioca flour

½ cup rice flour
2 tsp. baking powder
1 tsp. baking soda

Preheat oven to 375 degrees. Whip egg whites until stiff. Add egg yolks one at a time and then add fruit juice. Whip. Add dry ingredients; mix well. Bake 25 minutes in lightly greased loaf pan. Dough will not rise to top of pan.

Wedding Pancakes

This recipe was adapted from the pancake recipe offered by Bette Hagman in her cookbook, The Gluten-free Gourmet Cooks Fast and Healthy. *Pancakes are a carbohydrate. Serve with caution and watch portions.*

Pancake Mix
4 cups gluten-free flour mix
1 ½ tsp. salt
4 tsp. baking powder
2 tsp. baking soda
Mix ingredients in an airtight bowl and keep in freezer for future use.

To Make Pancakes
To 1 1/3 cups mix (above) add the following;
2 eggs
1 cup water
2 tsp. canola oil
3 whole nutmegs, grated
Grated corriander to taste
1 medium-size apple, peeled and grated

½ cup unsweetened applesauce (ingredients can only be water and apples)

Mix in large bowl. Do not overbeat. Spoon batter onto lightly greased pancake griddle and distribute batter evenly using the back of a spoon, if necessary. Cook until browned, then flip. Cook until browned.

Top with unsweetened applesauce and grated nutmeg, if desired.

Pie Crust

The following recipe is for a one-crust pie. I have had the best results by altering the mixture so that it resembles a traditional pie crust; that is, the mixture should look crumbly before adding just enough water to hold it together. If the mixture is not crumbly when the water is added, the crust tends to be crunchy rather than flaky, giving it a bit more of a bite than desired. This is an easy crust to make. It is adapted from Bette Hagman's, The Gluten-free Gourmet Cooks Fast and Healthy cookbook.

1 ½ cups light bean flour (recipe in this section)
1 tsp. baking powder
1 tsp. salt
1/3 cup canola oil
3-6 tbsp. cold water

Mix flour, baking soda, and salt. Mix in canola oil. Mixture should appear crumbly. If mixture is not crumbly, add more flour, one tablespoon at a time. When mixture appears crumbly, add just enough water to hold dough together.

Very lightly oil a 9" or 10" pie tin. Press mixture in pie tin by gently smoothing with the back of a spoon.

If the pie is to be filled and baked, pour the filling in gently and bake according to filling directions.

If the pie crust is to be baked then filled, bake the crust in a preheated oven at 400 degrees for 12-15 minutes, or until light brown. Cool completely before filling.

Fruit Pie Filling

Cooking pie fillings without sugar requires the use of very ripe fruit as the ripened fruit lends sweetness to the pie. It is possible to choose unripe fruit and wait for the fruit to ripen before preparing the filling. Whenever possible, wait for the fruit to be so ripe it is just ready to turn. That is the stage that makes the best pies.

You will find these fillings are not really formulas but a point in the right direction, lending themselves to other fruit and spice combinations. Add just a pinch of salt to enhance the natural sweetness, then cook the fruit on a very low simmer, bringing out the fruit's inherent sugar.

Apple Pie Filling

6-8 ripe apples (the sweetest you can find at the time)
Pinch of salt
Grated nutmeg to taste
Ground corriander to taste (if desired)
3-6 tbsp. water

Chop apples in small pieces and place in a pot. Add remaining ingredients (be conservative with the water and add more if necessary). Bring to boil, then reduce heat to very slow simmer. After apples have softened, approximately 30 minutes or so, taste filling and adjust spices, if desired. Simmer for 50-60 minutes, or until apples are tender and sweet. Place filling in an unbaked pie crust and bake for 40-50 minutes at 400 degrees, or until crust appears light brown. Cool completely before slicing.

Pear Pie Filling

6-8 ripe pears
Pinch of salt
Ground corriander to taste (if desired)
3-6 tbsp. water
Follow directions above.

Hot Apple Soup

4 green apples
4 McIntosh apples
2 ½ cups water
2 tbsp. lemon juice
½ tsp. grated nutmeg
1 cup almond milk (recipe in this section)

Dash of salt
Peel, core, and quarter apples. Combine all ingredients except almond milk in saucepan and bring to boil. Simmer 15 minutes or until apples are soft. Puree; return to pan; add almond milk and heat thoroughly, but don't boil. Serve with additional nutmeg, if desired.

Light Mayonaise

This recipe has been amended to meet our guidelines from Bette Hagman's cookbook, The Gluten-free Gourmet Cooks Fast and Healthy. Like all recipes I have tried from Ms. Hagman's cookbook, this is delicious. By experimenting with the seasonings, this may also make a nice dip for fresh vegetables or a topping for cooked asparagus.

1 ½ tsp. salt
½ tsp. dry mustard
3 tbsp. rice vinegar
1 cup water
¼ cup gluten-free flour mix
1 egg
1 ¼ cups canola oil

Place the salt, mustard, and vinegar in a deep, 1.5-quart mixing bowl and set aside.

In a small saucepan, blend the water slowly into the flour mix, stirring. Add egg. Cook over medium-low heat, stirring constantly, until the mixture simmers and becomes shiny and clear. Add to the ingredients in the mixing bowl.

Beat mixture with electric mixer while slowly adding oil. Continue beating mixture until mayonnaise is smooth, light colored, and thick. Refrigerate overnight before using.

Hummus Dip

Hummus dip is a thick, blonde dip that originated in the Middle East and is often served with pita bread. For our purposes, it is a great accompaniment to meat. It is also a nice dip for raw, organic vegetables.

2 cups garbanzo beans, cooked
2 tbsp. fresh parsley, snipped
1-2 tbsp. lemon juice
1 tbsp. canola oil
1 tbsp. water (more if necessary)
1-4 cloves garlic, pressed
Fresh cilantro, finely chopped, to taste

Salt to taste

Combine the first five ingredients in a food processor. Blend until smooth. Add remaining ingredients, adjusting to taste.

Makes 2 cups.

Seasoned Almonds

This recipe comes from the back of a package of Diamond Nut Company's whole almonds. It has been amended to meet our guidelines. For recipes or information from the Diamond Nut Company, contact them at: Diamond Nut Company of California, P. O. Box 1727, Dept. W, Stockton, CA 95201.

1 cup shelled Diamond almonds
1-2 tsp. canola oil
1 tsp. seasonings (your choice)

Spread almonds on baking sheet or in shallow pan. Toast at 350 degrees for 9-12 minutes, stirring several times. Toss toasted almonds with canola oil until evenly coated. Sprinkle with seasonings. Bake at 350 degrees for 3 minutes to allow seasonings to bake onto almonds. Cool. Store in airtight container or cool place. Makes one cup.

Almond Milk

We make almond milk quite a bit. It is easy and stores well in the refrigerator.

1/3 cup shelled almonds
2 cups water

Combine the ingredients in a blender. Blend on low setting at least one minute, or until the almonds have been ground into smaller, finer pieces. Blend another minute on medium speed. Blend one minute longer on high speed.

For very smooth almond milk, place a cheesecloth-covered collander over a medium-size bowl and pour contents of blender into collander (slowly or it will leak out the unlined edges). Pour almond milk into an airtight pitcher and refrigerate.

For less smooth almond milk, place a medium-size bowl under a collander that is not covered with cheesecloth, and repeat the above process.

Makes 2 cups.

Almond Milk Shake

An almond milk shake is a treat and can also be a great place to "hide" relatively tasteless supplements, such as digestive enzymes, alpha lipoic acid, chromium picolinate, zinc, magnesium, and calcium. Add the supplements to the shake while it is running and they will be blended smooth. If you add a room temperature banana to the almond milk, the shake will be thin and easy to drink through a straw. If you wish to have a thick, frosty shake, use a frozen banana instead. Remember, freezing fruit increases its sugar content and may cause a reaction. Based on Raja's recovery, we can now drink limited shakes, where at one time they caused reactions. Be wary of offering this too soon in your child's recovery. However, remember that as your child gets well, his body's tolerances will adjust. Raja can drink a small, fortified shake a day with no reactions as long as we adjust his other fruit intake accordingly.

In summertime, when the tree-ripened fruit is sweet and juicy, omit the carob, and try substituting your favorite fresh fruit for the banana.

Consider slicing and freezing some summertime fruit for the winter, as these shakes taste equally good year-round.

2 cups almond milk
1-2 bananas, fresh or frozen (see note below on freezing fruit)
Carob to taste (usually at least 3 heaping tbsp.)

Place all ingredients in a blender, and blend until smooth.

Note on freezing fruit: To freeze fruit, simply peel and place on plastic wrap, covering tightly, and place in freezer. For a nice treat on a hot day, place a popsicle stick in a banana (before covering with plastic wrap) and freeze, or cut bananas into slices and freeze on a tray. Delicious!

Homemade Juices

The following recipes are intended to represent a healthy option for special occasions such as birthday parties, where children and other guests might expect a sweet drink like soda or punch. These recipes are delicious, but are very sweet and could cause a reaction due to the large volume of fruit used to produce one serving. Consider diluting, or limiting your child to a very small portion, if you find he experiences reactions.

These recipes require a juicer. They came with The Juice Man Juicer, which is commonly available at department stores.

If you are hosting a party, consider making and refrigerating the juice ahead of time. Serve it in a punch bowl, floating ripe, organic strawberries on top and garnishing with fresh, organic mint leaves.

Watermelon Juice

Select a large, ripe, organic watermelon. Cut into strips and juice, rind and all.

Very refreshing on a hot summer day!

Lemonade

4 organic apples, with peel
¼ organic lemon, with peel
Slice apples so that they will fit in juicer tube. Juice apples and lemon into glass. Refrigerate, if desired. Makes one serving.

Pink Lemonade

4 organic apples, with peel
¼ organic lemon, with peel
6-8 ripe, organic strawberries
Slice apples so they will fit in juicer tube. Juice apples, lemon, and strawberries into glass. Refrigerate, if desired. Makes one serving.

Cranberry Sauce

I experimented with this recipe for the first time this holiday season and was pleased with the result. However, this version will not resemble traditional cranberry sauce (even if you are used to preparing your own) because the sauce does not gel much nor have the traditional sweet and sour taste. We call this the "Pink Sauce." Raja enjoys it so much he has to be stopped from eating too much.

1 12 oz. bag cranberries (seasonally available in produce section)
Juice of 5 oranges, plus pulp
2 Rome apples, peeled and chopped
½ tsp. corriander, ground
1 cup water
Dash salt

1 large, ripe banana, chopped small

Place water, salt, and cranberries in large pot and bring to boil. Reduce heat to simmer. Simmer cranberries while adding other ingredients. Continue stirring and cooking until all cranberries have popped and mixture is thickened and fairly smooth, about 30 minutes. Remove from heat and let stand or refrigerate.

Good warm or cold. Makes 6-8 servings.

Sweet Potatoes

This is a recipe that friends who are not on this diet have requested because they liked it so much. It is a simple dish and one we eat often. Although I normally cook the sweet potatoes in the microwave to save time, they can also be cooked in the oven which really brings out their sweet flavor. Yams appear to work equally well.

The leftovers are also delicious but don't be put off by the discoloration. Any part of the leftovers exposed to air will become brown, due to the bananas. This does not effect the flavor in any way.

This recipe is for one person. To increase the quantity, multiply by how many people you wish to feed. Additional potatoes may increase cooking time.

½-1 very ripe banana
Ground anise to taste
Salt to taste
1 medium micowaved or baked sweet potato.

Micowave or bake one medium sweet potato.

(To microwave, poke holes in potato with fork. Place in the microwave on high power for 6 minutes, checking for doneness with fork. If potato does not easily yield to fork when poked, additional cooking time is necessary. To bake, poke holes in potato and bake in oven on 350 degrees for 45-60 minutes, checking for doneness. If potato does not easily yield to fork when poked, additional cooking time is necessary).

Mash ½-1 ripe banana in bowl. Add cooked sweet potato and spices to taste. Serve while warm. Makes 1 regular or 2 small servings.

Carrot Salsa

If you like salsa, you may enjoy this one as much as I do. It reminds me of a similar salsa I ate at an authentic Mexican restaurant (where one orders at the counter and only in Spanish). It is a nice addition to a salad or other vegetables and is tasty on top of meat.

1 cup carrots, diced
1/3 cup tomato, diced
1 tbsp. canola or olive oil
1/3 cup green onions, sliced
1 clove garlic, pressed
Cilantro
Salt to taste

In a one-quart saucepan, combine carrots and oil. Cook over medium heat 5-7 minutes, or until carrots are tender, stirring frequently. Remove from heat. Add remaining ingredients. Mix well and cover. Chill at least 2 hours before serving.

Roxanne's Brown Rice Salad

This delicious recipe was e-mailed to me from my from my sister, Roxanne Nava, who has always had an appreciation for delicious and exotic food. This recipe is versatile, lending itself well to substitutions that fit personal taste. It has been amended to fit our guidelines.

5 cups short-grain brown rice, cooked
1 cup celery, finely chopped
1 cup carrots, finely chopped
1 cup apple, finely chopped
½ cup fresh parsley, minced
1 small red onion, finely chopped
2 cups chicken, cooked and chopped
In large bowl, mix ingredients well. Cover with dressing and refrigerate at least two hours or overnight.
Dressing:
½ cup canola oil
¼ cup rice vinegar
3 cloves garlic, pressed
Salt to taste
Seasonings to taste, if desired

Veggie-stuffed Zucchini

This is a nice dish for company because the presentation is attractive and the taste pleasing. Cooked squash, such a spaghetti or acorn squash, may be substituted with satisfactory results.
3 medium zucchini
1 ½ tsp.canola oil
1/3 cup chopped onion
2 cloves garlic, pressed
1 cup chopped, fresh mushrooms
1 medium tomato, chopped
Salt to taste

Pre-heat oven to 375 degrees. Cut zucchini in half lengthwise. Scoop out pulp, leaving ¼" hulls. Coarsely chop zucchini pulp. Set hulls and pulp aside.

Heat oil over medium heat in a medium skillet. Stir in onion and garlic. Cook 2-3 minutes, or until onion is crisp-tender, stirring frequently. Add zucchini and mushroom, cooking until tender. Remove from heat. Stir in tomato and season to taste.

Spoon mixture evenly into hulls. Place stuffed zucchini in 11"x 7" baking dish. Cover with foil and bake 25-30 minutes, or until hulls are crisp-tender.

Let stand 5 minutes before serving.

Roasted Carrots

This recipe is very simple and tasty. It was copied from the back of a bag of baby carrots purchased at the grocery store and amended to our guidelines.

16 ounces fresh California baby-cut carrots
1 small onion, cut in thin wedges
½ tbsp. canola oil
1 tbsp. chopped parsley
Salt to taste

Toss carrots and onion with oil. Arrange in a single-layer in a 13"x 9" baking pan, lightly coated with canola oil. Roast at 450 degrees, stirring occasionally, until carrots are lightly browned and just tender, about 20-25 minutes. Stir in parsley and salt to taste.

Makes four servings.

Gravy

This is a basic recipe for gravy, appropriate for meat or rice. Although sweet rice flour takes the place of cornstarch in this recipe, the gravy itself should mix and cook like traditional gravy; that is, when preparing it, slowly add the paste to the boiling mixture and whisk until smooth and thick. The type of liquid used gives the gravy its flavor. This recipe has been amended from the one offered on the back of the package of sweet rice flour and meets our specifications.

4 tbsp canola oil
1 ½ cups liquid or broth (water, vegetable, chicken, turkey, or beef)
¼ tsp. Salt
Over medium heat, bring the ingredients to a slow boil. While mixture is heating, make a paste using:
2 ½ tbsp. sweet rice flour
¼ cup liquid or broth (water, vegetable, chicken, turkey, or beef)

When mixture is boiling, slowly add paste to mixture, one tablespoon at a time. Stir over medium-low heat until thickened.

Swiss Chard Chicken

If you have never tried Swiss chard, you may be pleasantly surprised, especially if you try it in this dish. I found this recipe in the produce section of a grocery store. It has been adapted to fit our guidelines.

4 cups Swiss chard, washed and drained
Canola oil
1 cup onion, chopped
3 cloves garlic, pressed
12 ounces chicken breast meat, cubed
2 tbsp. water
1 cup rice, cooked
Salt to taste

Dice chard stems. Cut leaves into ½" strips. Place small amount of canola oil in skillet. Cook chard stems, onion, garlic, and chicken over medium heat for about 8 minutes. Add leaves and water; cook another 3 minutes, until chard stems are limp. Add rice. Salt to taste, cooking another 2 minutes.

Peanut Butter and Spice Rice

This recipe makes a great alternative to plain rice. The trick seems to be getting the peanut butter and spices in just the right proportion so the taste is delicious but not exactly identifiable.

Rice to serve four (follow manufacturer's directions)
1 tsp. peanut butter
¼ tsp. nutmeg, grated
¼ tsp. corriander, ground
Salt to taste

Following manufacturer's directions, add rice to water and stir to help prevent sticking. Add remaining ingredients, cover, and boil according to directions. Test for doneness before removing from heat as adding peanut butter has a tendency to increase cooking time.
Makes 4-6 servings.

Easy and Delicious Salad Dressing and Marinade

Here is another recipe that tends to get compliments from friends. In fact, this year I traded one gallon of this salad dressing for some great Thomas the Tank Engine artwork on Raja's comforter! Additionally, it is easy to add spices and get new combinations. I enjoy adding Herbs de Provence for a smooth flavor or oregano to shake it up a bit. Try the basic recipe and alter it as you wish.

Basic Recipe

Use any size container and adjust the amounts as necessary. In a cruet, I use about 6-8 cloves of pressed garlic and salt to taste.

Portion: 2/3 part canola oil
1/3 part rice vinegar
Pressed garlic to taste
Salt to taste

Place all ingredients in leak proof container and shake well. Adjust garlic and salt to taste. Use on salads, meats, or as a jerky marinade. Best marinade results achieved if allowed to marinate 24 hours or more.

Pesto

Just because we do not eat pasta does not mean we cannot eat pesto! Pesto is delicous on meat and can add a mild and savory flavor to cooked rice. It is very unlikely that pine nuts will cause a reaction, but prudence and careful observation are in order.

This recipe comes from a gorgeous cookbook, Sauces and Salsas, by Oded Schwartz. Mr. Schwartz has prepared many recipes that take little alteration to conform to our diet. This recipe has been altered to conform to our guidelines.

Although Mr. Schwartz notes that a more intense flavor is achieved by using a mortar and pestle to crush and blend the ingredients, I cheat by placing the ingredients in a blender and blend until smooth. If you wish to try the blender method, add the oil last, trickling it in a small, slow stream until a paste-like consistency is achieved. Adjust salt, if necessary. Undoubtedly, his tastes better, but if saving time is an issue, you may want to try the blender method.

2 large garlic cloves, halved and crushed with the flat side of a large knife

½ tsp. salt

½ cup pine nuts, dry roasted until golden brown (roasting instructions below)

4 cups fresh basil leaves

½ cup extra-virgin olive oil

By hand, put the garlic and salt in a heavy mortar and work to a paste with the pestle. Add the roasted pine nuts and continue pounding and mixing until smooth. Start adding the basil, a small handful at a time; pound and mix until smooth.

Slowly pour the olive oil in a steady stream and mix until it has a paste-like consistency. Add a little more salt to taste, if necessary. Serve immediately or transfer to sterile container.

Dry Roasted Pine Nuts

Place in a dry skillet over medium heat until they are lightly browned and beginning to give off an appetizing, spicy aroma. Be careful not to burn them—they are ready when they start to pop.

Easy Chicken Breasts with Marinade

This is a very fast and easy recipe; worth trying if your family enjoys chicken breasts.

Chicken breasts (one or more per person)

Canola oil

Prepared Easy and Delicious Salad Dressing and Marinade

Salt to taste

Place a small amount of canola oil in a skillet on medium-high heat. When oil is hot, place chicken breasts in skillet and brown on each side. While breasts are browning, generously baste with marinade. Turn chicken down to low heat to cook until done. Serve warm.

Basic Oven Jerky

Larry found this recipe on the Internet at <u>www.melborponsti.com</u> <u>/jerky/jerky081.htm</u>. Salting the meat generously while marinating has the greatest influence on the quality of the finished product. This recipe has been altered to conform to our guidelines.

1.5 lbs. lean, boneless meat (London broil works well)
¼ cup Easy and Delicious Salad Dressing and Marinade
Generous portion of salt
Chill meat in freezer until firm, but not frozen, about 30 minutes. Cut against the grain into strips.
Combine sliced meat and salad dressing in medium-sized pan, making certain all surfaces are covered. Generously cover with salt. Cover tightly and refrigerate overnight.

Place sliced meat on rack over pan. Dry meat in the oven at 150 degrees for 12 hours. Jerky is dried when it will crack, but not break, when bent.

Pork Loin Steak

2 lbs. pork loin steak
3 tbsp. canola oil
3 onions, finely chopped
1 clove garlic, pressed
1 cup ground almonds
Salt and seasonings to taste

Brown the meat in the oil. Season meat on both sides, then arrange in a baking dish.
Mix remaining ingredients and place over meat. Bake in 350 degree oven until tender, about 40 minutes.

Roasted Chicken

Roasted chicken is a main course we enjoy often. The fact that it bakes unattended for almost two hours frees up considerable time to do other things.

One whole chicken (be certain it is NOT injected with a solution)
Herbs de Provence seasoning mix (recipe follows)
Salt to taste
2 cloves garlic, pressed (optional)

Thoroughly wash chicken. Remove and discard contents from cavity. Place chicken on roasting pan, breast side down. If desired, place garlic inside chicken.

Using spice grinder, generously sprinkle outside of chicken with Herbs de Provence seasoning mix. Salt to taste.

Bake in 350 degree oven for 1 hour and 45 minutes, or until meat near the breastbone is no longer pink.

Herbs de Provence Seasoning Mix

This is wonderful mix that I tend to use on everything. The taste is calming and savory. Herbs can be purchased in bulk rather inexpensively, especially at major health food chain stores such as Whole Foods or Wild Oats markets.

Using equal parts of the herbs listed below, place in medium-size bowl and mix thoroughly. Place mixture in spice grinder. Store remaining mixture in an airtight container, such as a canning jar, for future use.

Marjoram
Oregano
Rosemary
Savory
Thyme

Goulash

Goulash is an easy meal that mixes up in minutes if cooked rice is available. Goulash can be an effective way to slip some vegetables into your child's diet, especially if the vegetables are diced very small. This also makes a nice stuffing for cooked acorn or spaghetti squash.

One or more pounds ground beef (as lean or fat as you prefer)
Canola oil
2-4 white, yellow, or purple onions, chopped fine
1-4 cloves garlic, pressed
1 zucchini, finely chopped
1 summer squash, finely chopped
½ cup carrots, finely chopped
1 or more cups rice, cooked
Herbs de Provence seasoning mix, ground (see Roasted Chicken for recipe)
Salt to taste

In a large skillet, brown the onions and garlic in the canola oil over medium heat until tender. Add ground beef. Separate into tiny pieces while cooking. Cook thoroughly. Unless excessively oily, do not drain.

Add vegetables. Cook over medium-low heat until vegetables are soft. Add rice. Serve immediately.

Hearty Beef Stew

I feel that two spices inevitably make a stew hearty and delicious: oregano and cardamon. Cardamon is a very pungent spice; a little goes a long way toward flavoring a large pot of stew. Cardamon combines well with oregano, which I use with reckless abandon, and tinker around with anything else that conforms to our guidelines.

Enough stew meat to feed the family for one or more meals
Canola oil
Water
Plenty of onions (any kind), quartered
Plenty of garlic
Plenty of vegetables, excluding potatoes
Plenty of salt
Plenty of oregano
2 pods cardamon seeds (remove seeds from pods and discard pods)

Any other spice that smells like it would make a good addition to the pot

In a skillet over medium heat, brown stew meat in canola oil, turning when browned. Add onions and garlic, browning lightly with meat.

When meat is browned, transfer to stew pot. Add enough water to bring water level to the halfway mark. Add vegetables and seasonings. Bring to boil.

Once stew is boiling, cover and reduce heat to low, simmering 2-3 hours, or until meat falls apart when pressed with fork.

Breakfast Scramble

This is an easy breakfast that quickly adapts to any mealtime preference by adding vegetables or varying spices.

1 lb. Ground beef(as fat or lean as yoou prefer)
Canola oil
2-4 onions, finely chopped
1-2 cloves garlic, pressed (if desired)
4 eggs
Salt and seasonings to taste

In a large skillet, brown onions and garlic in canola oil over medium heat until onions are carmelized. Add ground beef, breaking into fine pieces while cooking. Stir and flip constantly.

When beef is thoroughly cooked, add eggs directly into beef mixture and stir quickly to evenly distribute, as if scrambling. Add salt and seasonings to taste. Cook until eggs are done. Serve immediately.

Mock Sausage

This recipe is from the cookbook, Good Food, Milk Free, Grain Free *by Hilda Cherry Hills. I highly recommend this cookbook, as much for the information as for the recipes. The author is extremely knowledgeable regarding the connection between food and food-induced reactions. In the first page of her cookbook, Ms. Hills states that,*

"One in five people in Britain today [1980] will suffer from some form of mental illness. It is known that certain factors in food can worsen these conditions but that by following a diet from which foods containing the harmful factors are excluded the condition may be alleviated or even cured provided that the diet is rigidly adhered to."

This cookbook provides many recipes requiring little or no alternation as well as in-depth information from one who has been pursuing the connection between wellness and food-induced reactions.

¾ lb. raw, lean beef
1 egg, beaten
½ cup cooked sweet potato
1/3 tsp. crushed herbs (Herbs de Provence would work well here)
Salt as required

The night before, mince the beef, then stir in the potato, herbs, and salt. Pound to a paste with the beaten egg and pack into a straight-sided jar about two-and-a-half inches across. Leave in the refrigerator until the next morning. Slice and fry like commercial sausage meat.

About the Author

Michelle Cheney is a wife, mother, and holistic massage therapist who lives with her husband and son in the United States.

What ended as a book began as a personal journey to help her son recover from autism. Stunned by the realization that her son's developmental disorder was the largely the result of physical pain and cognitive disruption stimulated by food and environmental substances, she wished to communicate her findings to others. She contacted doctors at separate, well-funded programs dedicated to researching autism and informed them of her discoveries. Knowing her testimony would be considered anecdotal, she still hoped that they would understand the urgency of such information and begin testing for efficacy. To her disappointment, the doctors did not respond. Feeling an urgent need to communicate this information with interested parents, she wrote a book encompassing both her findings and the approach she employed to facilitate her son's recovery.

Michelle is dedicated to assisting those who wish to help children recover from autism. She may be contacted by e-mail in care of *jaragon2000@aol.com*, or at:

P. O. Box 146
Pope Valley, CA 94567
(707) 928-4588

Appendix

In the Introduction, I stated that the approach to autism recovery outlined herein is based on my belief that autism is a progressive, systemic, allergic response and that this approach could be successfully implemented, and results achieved, without fully understanding the rational behind this theory. However, since the observations and research that led to this conclusion support the theoretical framework on which this approach rests, they are included for review. It is my intention to offer complete information including terminology and methodology that we may share common references for testing theoretical efficacy.

The theory that diagnosable autism represents the cumulative effect of progressive, systemic, allergic responses to dietary and environmental stimuli is based on patterns that I have observed and documented. Please remember that a pattern represents a set of symptoms observed and documented a minimum of three times. This means that a process had to occur on at least three separate occasions and manifest the same symptoms for the same duration with the same results before considering such occurrence representative of a pattern.

This theory was created from hindsight by comparing and contrasting Raja's recovery and regression after a stable state was achieved. Rather than formulating and testing hypotheses in advance, numerous and unexpected behavioral symptoms encountered during the early phase of recovery made this theory possible. By creating and maintaining a stable state then observing and documenting the disruption of a stable state and corresponding behavioral symptoms, it was possible to hypothesize and research correlates with the symptoms noted during disruption.

Such disruptions were termed "reactions." Reactions were opportunities to further my understanding of autism by comparing and contrasting symptoms to those observed in a stable state. Moreover, many aspects of reactions were tangible, producing symptoms that could be observed, documented, and timed. When three or more reactions had produced observably similar symptoms in intensity, duration, and behavioral manifestations, a pattern was concluded. Emerging patterns produced opportunities for further hypotheses. Research was used to validate or nullify the efficacy of hypotheses until a theory emerged.

Influencing Mainstream Medical and Psychological Communities

Although I have endeavored to simplify this theory as much as possible, it has been researched and written with the hope of attracting the interest and attention of mainstream medical and psychological communities for several reasons. First, I am hopeful that the mainstream medical and psychological communities who receive funding to research autism may consider this theory plausible and choose to test the theoretical efficacy of this approach. As a parent of an autistic child, I was given verbal and written material regarding autism that had been generated by mainstream medical and/or psychological sources. Such material appeared to constitute the information used and disseminated by doctors and therapists to educate themselves, and parents, regarding autism. While the material provided facts and definitions, it did not offer explanations regarding the developmental degeneration that characterized Raja's entrance into diagnosable autism. Moreover, the professionals to whom I turned for answers used material produced by mainstream medical and psychological sources to further their understanding of autism, so their breadth of understanding was generally no greater than mine. To make matters worse, the material also described autism as a mysterious and hopeless disorder for which there is no known cause or cure.

Second, while I have experienced autism as a mysterious disorder, I have never believed it was hopeless. However, without the interest of the mainstream medical and psychological communities, this approach and the theoretical framework on which it rests will remain a grassroots outreach project. While I believe that even a grassroots outreach project is well worth the effort it took to produce this text, considerable recovery time is lost when parents must research healing interventions using grassroots sources. It would be preferential to receive information regarding healing resources upon completion of diagnosis at a mainstream testing facility. It breaks my heart to realize that Raja could have started making developmental gain when he was evaluated as developmentally delayed, potentially avoiding diagnosable autism altogether, had I been informed of an approach such as this upon completion of the initial evaluation. Therefore, it is of utmost importance to attract the interest and attention of mainstream medical and psychological researchers because the interventions they test, endorse, and publish represent the vast majority of printed literature available to educate parents and professionals alike.

Finally, the greatest reason I am hopeful to attract the interest and attention of mainstream medical and psychological researchers is that parents and professionals may otherwise miss the critical opportunity to understand that autistic children are in physical pain. Many antisocial and enigmatic behaviors displayed by autistic children are the result of considerable physical pain triggered by contact with allergens. Contact with allergens produces chemical reactions resulting in tissue swelling that causes pain. Unabated physical pain is complicated by the child's inability to articulate such pain and the parent's inability to understand the source of such pain. Unfortunately, until autism is studied holistically, manifestations of antisocial and unusual behaviors may only be considered brain dysfunction. Children suffering the painful physical repercussions of systemic allergic response will continue to suffer in silence while parents, teachers, and therapists continue to wring their hands, doing the best they can with difficult circumstances and inadequate information.

While this theory is articulated for the benefit of interested parents, it is my sincerest wish that it may also be considered plausible by mainstream medical and psychological communities researching autism. To this end, I largely contained my research to traditional literature regarding allergies. Thus, I have compared the observed and documented symptoms of reactions to those described in mainstream medical literature. Furthermore, I have attempted to understand and articulate the function of the immune system using traditional medical models. For example, when describing autism's theoretical complement cascade, I have based this paradigm on the immune system's complement cascade offered by literature produced by the National Institute of Health.

Although I am not a physician, I do consider myself a good detective. The theory presented herein has been deduced by viewing autism holistically, considering both physical and cognitive symptoms as separate manifestations of the same disorder. Every attempt has been made to *connect* symptoms that are often scrutinized separately because my experience with Raja, as well as related research and conversations with other parents of autistic children, indicates that afflicted individuals manifest similar symptoms both physically and cognitively. Additionally, all behavioral symptoms have been scrutinized holistically and are considered synergistic manifestations of the physical and cognitive changes resulting from exposure to dietary and environmental allergens that induce reactions.

Formulating the Theory

Two experiences were critical to the formulation of this theory. First, I had to be introduced to the concept of food-induced reactions and see for myself the negative impact food had on Raja's cognition and demeanor. As you many recall, I was introduced to the concept of food-induced reactions in a magazine article entitled, "We Cured Our Son of Autism." In this article, author Karyn Seroussi outlined the relationship between casein, gluten, and autistic behavior. Using a casein-free, gluten-free diet and limited therapies, Seroussi facilitated her autistic son's recovery in 18 months. Although Seroussi had made it very clear that it was necessary to eliminate *all* exposure to casein and gluten, I had a hard time believing that diet could be a factor in Raja's autism until I experienced for myself the diet-related changes in Raja. This occurred while studying for my college exams, when Raja ate large quantities of foods containing casein and gluten that he normally ate only in small quantities. By the end of exam week, Raja was aggressive, unable to process or attend a verbal request, and laid down on the floor in a department store. Observing the dramatic change in Raja's demeanor and behavior allowed me to experientially verify the relationship between diet and autistic manifestations.

The second critical experience in formulating this theory occurred with my husband, Larry. Although he has not been tested and diagnosed, Larry demonstrates many typical, autistic tendencies. For instance, Larry is not expressive or social and feels anxious in a crowd, even if it is a crowd of people he knows. Larry prefers not to talk if it is not necessary. He tells me it is difficult to keep up in a conversation, finding himself unable to switch subjects with ease. Larry thrives on repetition and routine, noticeably shaken by change. Larry cannot comprehend concepts or abstract thought, needing mechanical or formulaic explanations to foster understanding (e.g., First A, then, B, then C, etc.). Larry has not had a close friend since elementary school and works well on the periphery of relationships. In his family of origin, Larry describes himself as, "An outsider looking in." Through observation and interviews, I have long believed that Larry is autistic.

Just as it was necessary for me to believe that a relationship *could* exist between food and food-elicited reactions, it was necessary for me to conclude that Larry *could be* autistic before examining the relationship between his autism and his reactions. In other words, based on the premise that Larry *could be* autistic, his food-induced reactions would be of particular interest and would represent something universal in the autistic spectrum. As you may remember, Larry and Raja are not biologically related, negating the genetic link between symptoms similarly manifested by each of them during reactions. I have observed and documented patterns of food and environmentally induced reactions that manifest similar symptoms in each of them. Moreover, the food and environmental substances that induce reactions in Larry and Raja do not induce reactions in me. Since Larry and Raja are not related, and since I have observed and documented them reacting to the same food and environmental factors, it was the *factors*, not the *genetics*, that bore further investigation.

Like Raja, Larry had achieved and maintained a stable state for some time before experiencing his first reaction. It was Larry's first "known" reaction because it was the first occasion he had ever timed, documented, and described the conditions of reaction occurring in his body. Although he remembered experiencing the symptoms of reaction countless times throughout his lifetime, he had never understood that what he had experienced on those occasions was a reaction. By achieving, maintaining, and violating a stable state, the seemingly unrelated symptoms of reaction became different parts of the same process known as a reaction.

I had asked Larry to document and describe the sensations related to his reaction because Raja had manifested symptoms of a reaction 90 minutes prior; thus, they were both having reactions at almost the same time (Raja was 90 minutes ahead of Larry). I hoped that Larry's ability to articulate his experiences would help me understand Raja's behavior. When Larry began to describe the sensations associated with reaction, such as excessive thirst and tingling that prevented him from sitting still, I observed similarities in Raja that had heretofore gone unexplained. Although Raja's symptoms occurred sooner and were more pronounced than Larry's, Raja and Larry seemed to be experiencing the same sensations based on Larry's descriptions and Raja's manifestations. For three days, the sensations associated with reaction continued unfolding, effecting each of them physically, cognitively, emotionally, behaviorally, and socially. On the fourth day, each of them appeared to be cleared of symptoms and functioned unimpaired.

When the unexpected incident was finally over, I believed I had just witnessed a snapshot of autism in the making. I reasoned that if one unexpected reaction produced a single snapshot, a series of snapshots taken in rapid progression would produce a moving picture. Using this premise for further investigation, I began to document Raja's reactions and asked Larry to do the same with his. When the same sensations occurred with the same frequency for the same duration three times in one individual, a pattern was concluded. When the patterns were compared, definite similarities emerged.

It should be noted that reactions were always unexpected and never intentionally induced. During Larry's first documented reaction, at which time Raja was also manifesting symptoms of a reaction, suffering was noted physically, cognitively, emotionally, behaviorally, and socially, making induced reactions inconceivable. Moreover, in the early phase of this approach, it was unfortunately easy to find stimuli that induced reactions, often inducing a new reaction shortly after recovery was completed. Although every precaution was taken to avoid reactions, this approach was developed from trial and error by locating and subsequently avoiding substances that produced reactions. I would never suggest or allow an induced reaction because developmental gain appears to cease during reactions. The daily breakdown of symptoms occurring during reactions will be described in detail later. Although the symptoms of reaction are only described in relation to food, both Larry and Raja have experienced reactions to environmental stimuli, including so little as bubble bath *residue* on another child's toys.

Larry's reactions, and his ability to articulate, time, and document the various stages, gave me a unique and educational window into the process that results in diagnosable autism. Each reaction represented a three-day healing process, during which time the symptoms would move and change throughout his body, clearing on the fourth day. However, every time he had a reaction, the symptoms and progression were the same. Each reaction began the same way, starting with recognizable symptoms reported during the previous reaction, moving through his body at the same rate and in the same progression. Comparing manifestations of Larry's reactions to manifestations of Raja's reactions provided opportunities to hypothesize similarities in all aspects of reactions, although this could not be verified by asking Raja because he was pre-verbal. Nonetheless, by comparing manifestations and allowing for differences in developmentally appropriate means of expression, I concluded that Larry and Raja were experiencing similar symptoms and that reactions represented a patterned response. Furthermore, the patterned response produced a progressive, systemic chain of events requiring three days to heal for every one exposure, during which time developmental gain ceased. As this paradigm unexpectedly emerged over and over again, I began researching the symptoms in relation to other diseases to gain further understanding.

After observing the reaction and healing pattern repeat itself on three separate occasions, I suspected allergy. Many of Larry's symptoms were similar to symptoms reported by those suffering with pollen allergies, including dry throat, runny nose, sinus swelling, and sinus pain. While researching allergies, I encountered information regarding anaphylaxis. Surprisingly, I found many similarities between anaphylactic symptoms and those documented and described by Larry while experiencing a reaction. Moreover, many typical anaphylactic symptoms are also common in autistic individuals whose profiles have been described in conversation or literature. Ultimately, the similarity of symptoms between those manifested in Larry's reactions and those described in anaphylactic reactions led me to theorize that the behavioral indicators manifesting as diagnosable autism are actually the cumulative effects of a progressive, systemic, allergic response. The similarities between anaphylaxis and autism will be discussed shortly.

Theory

The theory outlined herein posits that the behavioral changes resulting in diagnosable autism represent the cumulative effect of disruptions in physical and cognitive processes stimulated by allergens in food and environmental substances that produce a progressive, systemic, immune response. This progressive, systemic, immune response lasts three days. As new allergens are contacted during the three days required for recovery, physical and cognitive processes become disrupted. Over time, daily allergen contact minus necessary recovery time results in observable behavioral manifestations. Eventually, the disrupted physical and cognitive processes resulting in behavioral manifestations become diagnosable autism.

In order to create common understanding of this framework, I have striven to provide definitions for unfamiliar terminology as well as thorough and accurate documentation regarding critical observations and conclusions. We will begin with a daily description of the patterned symptoms occurring during a reaction as individually manifested by Larry and Raja. We will then consider allergic response as perpetuated in the immune system by an allergen and the similarities between anaphylactic symptoms and patterned reactions manifested by Larry and Raja. We will compare the immune system's complement cascade with autism's theoretical complement cascade and how cellular memory makes it possible to identify foods that trigger reactions by touch. Finally, we will discuss possibilities regarding why foods that trigger reactions become addictive, why addictive food leads to a self-limited diet, and how the cumulative effect of reactions can manifest as diagnosable autism.

Let us begin with a description of the patterned symptoms occurring individually in Larry and Raja during a reaction. The manifestations are categorized by day and by individual.

Please remember that the descriptions of Larry's manifestations include my observations as well as his documented and described conditions. The descriptions of Raja's manifestations are based on observation only as he was pre-verbal in the early phase of intervention and unable to speak or indicate a negative or affirmative response to a question.

Day One Symptoms of Reaction—Raja

Raja begins demonstrating symptoms of a reaction 90 minutes after his meal. His sudden, pronounced, and atypical behavior is the initial manifestation of a reaction. He drinks a lot of water. He becomes hyperactive. His eyes dilate. His mood is temporarily elated. He cannot listen or stay on task. He demonstrates reckless social behavior, such as slapping a stranger on the stomach (something he has never done except during a reaction). His motor skills are clumsy. He demonstrates a high pain tolerance (e.g., he bumped into a table very hard and barely cried). He frequently lays down on the ground or floor. He constantly moves from one activity to another, engaging in any given activity less than two minutes. These initial symptoms last three hours.

When initial symptoms elapse, Raja is normally tired and often falls asleep. During sleep, Raja's breathing is very shallow. I must get very close to him to determine he is breathing at all. His sleep is quite restless, characterized by tossing, turning, kicking, and frequent waking spells, during which time he may get up and drink water. His cheeks are flushed. Perspiration forms around his hairline.

Day Two Symptoms of Reactions—Raja

Upon waking, Raja's mood is cool and aloof (he normally awakens smiling and happy). He wants to eat immediately after getting up. His gait is stiff and tight-legged, often walking on his tip-toes. He opens his mouth very wide while simultaneously holding his arms behind him and opening and clenching his hands. Overall, his mood is impatient, grumpy, and anti-social, as if he would prefer not to be bothered. He may manifest aggravation, frustration, or displeasure over minute details. He cannot stay on task or exercise follow-through. He must be asked repeatedly to execute a request, including a simple one that he can easily perform otherwise. His eye contact is severely diminished or absent. His tactile defensiveness is quite pronounced, constantly squirming and/or crying while his teeth are being brushed.

Raja craves apples, easily eating one after another, if allowed. Overall, he becomes fixated on food, eating every 20-30 minutes. Going to the grocery store is very difficult, as he demands to eat forbidden snack foods such as donuts, candy, or chips. When denied such foods, he demonstrates extreme displeasure, including crying, screaming, kicking and/or lying down on the floor. His fixated behavior is repetitious, constantly demanding foods I have just explained that he cannot have. Less than 60 seconds can elapse before he will again indicate that he wants a food I have denied. This can generate more fits of displeasure as described above. His sleep is very restless, frequently tossing, turning, kicking, and waking frequently. He appears to get more comfortable by putting pressure on his feet by pushing hard against something, which he does frequently in his sleep.

Day Three Symptoms of Reaction—Raja

Upon waking, Raja's mood is warmer than Day Two, but still not normal. Raja cannot stay on task or exercise follow-through, requiring attention nearly every moment. When he does something inappropriate, he is very reluctant to stop his behavior. I cannot use the normal cues in eliciting appropriate behavior. For instance, Raja knows the phrase, "That's not ours" to exercise respect for other people's things. Normally, he hears the phrase and responds appropriately by refraining from touching the indicated object. However, on Day Three, he cannot incorporate the normal cues and curb his behavior. When he is denied, he expresses his displeasure in ways similar to Day Two but with less intensity.

Raja walks on his tip-toes occasionally, exercising the same facial and hand gestures as on Day Two, although with less frequency. His eye contact improves. By the time he is ready for bed, he is cooperative. His sleep pattern is within normal limits.

Day Four Symptoms of Reaction—Raja

Raja is happy upon waking, smiling and hugging me. Instead of looking for food, he looks for toys that interest him. His tic-like behavior has diminished to normal levels. His eye contact returns to normal levels. His attention span and ability to execute a request return to normal levels. His social interaction returns to normal levels. On Day Four, all behavioral indicators of a reaction cease. Raja appears to have reached homeostasis as indicated by behaviors in normal levels for all types of activities, including cognition and demeanor.

Day One Symptoms of Reaction—Larry

Larry's reports manifesting symptoms of a reaction three hours after finishing the same food eaten by Raja. His first symptom is a dry throat. The second sign is pain in his lower back, which appears to be in the kidney area. Then his whole body tingles, which he describes as a pleasant sensation, a sort of a "buzz" all over his whole body. As the buzz wears off, his sinuses swell and his muscles tighten, followed by a feeling of being on edge. While he is feeling edgy, his joints get sore. His urine has a strong smell. His sleep is restless. He awakened six times during the night, reporting feeling hot, uncomfortable, and achy all over. He is thirsty and gets out of bed to drink water. He is unable to find a comfortable sleeping position that allows him to rest.

What I notice about Larry on Day One is that while he is tingling, he is exceptionally happy for a short while. He is very talkative and constantly fidgeting, whether rocking back and forth from one foot to the other, or moving his jaw from side to side. He does not keep constant eye contact, looking around a lot without appearing to pay attention to anything, even while participating in conversation. He appears to want to do something, but does not actually do anything but keep moving. His cheeks are flushed. His eyes are dilated. He is capable of staying on task for only a short period but is easily distracted, He is beginning to become fixated on food and eating.

Day Two Symptoms of Reaction—Larry

Upon waking, Larry reports that his whole body is hurting. His knees and elbows have pronounced pain, making movement difficult. Everything is a struggle. He does not want to do anything, even things he would normally do. He experiences a strange sensation in his stomach, like a low-grade nausea, constantly searching for food to help ameliorate his stomach discomfort. Food cravings begin (he says he is looking for something but doesn't know what). He begins snacking every 20-30 minutes. He is unusually attracted to snack foods at the grocery store. He has a difficulty passing up candy, popcorn, and potato chips. He eats as many as five or more apples, craving them similar to junk food.

He finds it hard to pay attention. He doesn't want to be around other people. He wants to be left alone. He says he is hypersensitive about odors. He describes the feeling as having his face shoved into a frying pan while food is being cooked—that food and others smells are very strong and temporarily overwhelm him. His sleep is restless but he awakens less frequently than Day One. He reports feeling hot while waking during the night.

What I notice about Larry on Day Two is he wakes up appearing tired. His initial demeanor is grumpy. Throughout the day, his demeanor is angry, curt, rude, and sarcastic. His tone of voice is cold and mean. Anything out of the ordinary is downright distasteful and he protests at nearly everything. His gait is very stiff, nearly walking in his tip-toes. He is constantly stretching, moving his neck, back, and fingers. He acts as though he wants to be left alone.

He is incapable of making choices or finding solutions, even if they are immediately at hand. For instance, I asked him to go to the grocery store and purchase a specified amount of ground beef. He brought back a package that was too large. When I asked why he purchased such a large package of meat, he said it was the smallest one they had. When I asked if he had checked at the meat counter not five feet away, he said it never even occurred to him. That is typical of Day Two. If I do not tell him specifically what to do and how to do it, he cannot be self-directed in any way.

Day Three Symptoms of Reaction—Larry

Larry reports feeling like he is in a fog sometimes. He describes small noises as being very loud, such as the hum of florescent lights or the refrigerator motor. He says background noises seem very loud and often annoying. He reports feeling a little achy and stiff. He stretches periodically throughout the day. His sleep is restful. He does not awaken during the night.

What I notice about Larry on Day Three is that he is grumpy upon waking. He is still fixated on food and has food cravings. Much of our conversation revolves around food. He still has a hard time entering a grocery store, stopping to drool over the snacks. He is largely self-involved, appearing not to care or inquire about those around him. He will only complete tasks if I ask repeatedly and check to see that he has completed them. Moreover, he may complete tasks when asked but may not complete them correctly. For instance, he puts the dishes away but does not put them back in the right place.

Additionally, his judgment is 100% wrong sometimes. For example, we were driving through a town unfamiliar to him. He was operating the vehicle; I was giving directions. I instructed him to turn left at the stop sign. He stopped at the stop sign, then proceeded to turn right. Puzzled, I asked him if he heard me tell him left. He replied, "Yes." Then he said *he actually thought he was going left*, silently questioning himself after I questioned him aloud. This example of absence of judgment is not an isolated incident on Day Three. Day Three is characterized by a frightening reversal of judgment.

Toward the end of the evening of Day Three, Larry's listening skills are returning, as is a genuine interest in things other than self. His food fixation appears to be diminishing. His competency is almost fully restored. He can easily accomplish tasks without constant reminders or supervision. His demeanor is patient, kind, and gentle, but slightly removed. He has the ability to hold cursory, reciprocal conversations as long as the duration is short.

Day Four Symptoms of Reaction—Larry

Upon awakening, Larry reports feeling good. Specifically, he says he feels alive. He is not experiencing any pain. He does not need a shower to wake up. He is not hungry upon waking. He slept soundly without waking during the night.

What I notice about Larry on Day Four is that he alert and aware. He appears to be feeling good. He is capable of being playful, thoughtful, and helpful. His judgment returns. He stays on task and exercises follow-through. Noises and smells are not disruptive. His mood is constant. He smiles. Food cravings are gone, as is preoccupation with self.

Correlation of Behavioral Indicators During Reaction

There is a strong correlation between Larry's described and observed symptoms during a reaction and behavioral manifestations indicating symptoms of reaction in Raja. Although Raja's behavior is more severe and age-appropriate, many of the behavioral indicators of reaction correspond with those described by, or observed in, Larry.

For example, at first sign of reaction, both Larry and Raja appear very thirsty and drink a lot of water. Both have heightened elation for a short period of time. Neither have the ability to sit still for more than a moment. Both demonstrate an inability to stay on task, follow directions, or exercise follow-through. Both have difficulty sleeping through the night. Both appear to have food cravings, constantly eating every 20-30 minutes. Both crave apples, eating one after another, if allowed. Both are irritable and aloof. Both appear to be sore on Day Two. While Larry describes feeling sore and has a very stiff gait, constantly moving and stretching, Raja exhibits considerable tic-like behavior and stands on his tip-toes frequently. Both have dilated eyes and flushed cheeks. Both appear to be hot during sleep. While Larry describes feeling hot and uncomfortable, Raja develops perspiration around his hairline and gets out of bed to drink water. Although Raja's symptoms of reaction appear earlier than Larry's, their symptoms appear to be systemic, closely linked, and triggered by the same substances.

Developmental Gain Ceases During a Reaction

A reaction appears to trigger a chain of events manifesting symptoms physically, emotionally, cognitively, socially, and behaviorally. The body and mind appear to be effected systemically and simultaneously, such that while the body is experiencing physical pain, the mind is undergoing cognitive changes as well. Overwhelmed by the process of recovery, even normal tasks are difficult. Attention span is severely diminished. Preoccupation with food is paramount. Hypersensitivity to smells and sounds is apparent, as well as increased tactile defensiveness. Judgment is reversed. Consumed by uncontrollable changes altering everything from perception to sensation, developmental gain appears to cease.

Perhaps the greatest discovery is that a reaction results in physiological changes that are painful and that the pain caused by the physiological changes occurring during a reaction also effects demeanor. Autistic children are always described as having limited social and learning abilities. What we don't know is that their limited social and learning abilities could largely be due to the physical pain they are experiencing resulting from reactions. It must be very difficult to be focused and social while one's body is effectively under siege.

When Larry's first symptoms of reactions appeared, I asked him to describe them to me hoping it would help me understand Raja more effectively. On Day Two, when Larry explained that his body was undergoing painful transformations and that these painful transformations had also resulted in sleep deprivation, waking him as many as six times during the night, I immediately realized that Raja's unpleasant demeanor and interrupted sleep could be due to pain, too. Suddenly, when Larry said he was hurting all over, I made a connection to Raja's behavior and knew that everything from walking on his tip-toes to his insistence on routine was a response to his physical agony. I am greatly indebted to Larry for his ability to articulate the symptoms of reaction. The realization that autistic children are in a constant state of physical pain dramatically increased my understanding of why they do what they do, however inexplicable it may seem. I imagine how hard it would be to concentrate, execute a command, or be responsive to another human being if my whole body were hurting. It would be like constantly having the flu—achy, irritated, and in need of compassionate attention and help. From this perspective, all enigmatic autistic behaviors become understandable, and the efforts to prevent contact with food or environmental substances that cause reactions become sacred acts of love.

After observing and documenting the symptoms of reactions occurring for both Raja and Larry on three separate occasions, a pattern was concluded. Upon conclusion of a pattern, research was conducted regarding similarities between symptoms of reaction and symptoms of other known diseases. I suspected allergy due to the number of similarities between Larry's symptoms and those described by acquaintances suffering with pollen allergies. Although there is relatively little information regarding allergies per se, allergy research inevitably led to an explanation of the immune system because it is the immune system that is impacted when encountering the allergens responsible for allergies. Additionally, it was during this research that I encountered information regarding anaphylaxis. Immediately, the presence of several similarities became apparent between Larry's reactions and anaphylactic reactions. The results of that research will be described shortly.

In order to further an understanding of the parallels between anaphylaxis and Larry's reaction, we will begin with a cursory understanding of the immune system and an allergic response.

The Immune System and Allergic Response

What we refer to as the immune system is not actually a "system" located somewhere in the body but a network of organs, glands, and cells that function to keep us in a dynamic state of wellness by removing foreign invaders such as antigens and allergens. An antigen is any substance that can trigger an immune response (1). An allergen is an antigen that not only triggers an immune response, but sensitizes an individual such that subsequent encounters with the same allergen instigate a flood of chemicals producing symptoms such as sinus swelling, runny nose, and itching (2). An allergic response results from contact with an allergen. An allergic response is considered a disorder of the immune system (3).

When the immune system encounters an antigen, a complex but non-disruptive process ensues whereby the antigen is located, isolated, destroyed, and eliminated. This process occurs countless times throughout the day and is considered non-disruptive because it does not produce symptoms such as those experienced with an allergic reaction. Thus, our immune systems are constantly working to rid our bodies of foreign matter, accomplishing this mighty task without producing symptoms that would alert us to the changes occurring within our bodies.

However, when the immune system encounters an allergen, it responds with the intention of removing foreign matter but additionally produces unpleasant symptoms that alert us to the immune response occurring within our bodies. The normally non-disruptive immune response becomes a disruptive response, producing uncomfortable symptoms, such as congestion or runny nose, demanding our attention.

The very nature of an allergic response is progressive. After exposure, for reasons not yet understood, an allergen sensitizes and individual to its presence such that subsequent exposures result in an allergic response (4). Often, an allergic response creates measurable antibodies that are produced in the course of arresting and eliminating the allergen (5). The presence of measurable antibodies is the means by which traditional allergists determine allergy (6). Although many doctors estimate that two-thirds of cases involving allergic symptoms do not produce measurable antibodies, reactions produced by pollen, asthma, and anaphylaxis do, allowing the mainstream medical community to validate them as allergic reactions through measurement (7).

Comparing Symptoms of Reaction to Anaphylaxis

In a paper published by the American Academy of Allergy, Asthma, and Immunology (AAAAI), anaphylaxis is described as a 'systemic reaction' that effects "some people after they are exposed to a substance to which they are severely allergic," resulting in symptoms such as nausea, cramps, swelling of tissues and joints, severe anxiety, sneezing, itchy throat, nasal congestion, diarrhea, a feeling of warmth and flushing, and loss of consciousness, among others (8).

For Larry and Raja, many symptoms of reaction are similar to those noted in anaphylaxis. In Larry's case, his symptoms begin with a dry throat, then move to back pain around the kidney area. He then feels tingling all over, which is initially experienced as pleasant but becomes painful as the tingling resides, giving way to stiffness. His sinuses become congested. He describes the congestion as similar to that of a sinus cold. He becomes hot. He has joint pain that is especially pronounced in his knees and elbows. He aches all over, subsiding over time. His mental capacities are impaired. Both Larry and Raja have symptoms of warmth and flushing, such feeling hot, frequently drinking water, and visibly red cheeks. Both of them demonstrate anxiety being around others. Both of them have prolonged food cravings related to what Larry describes as a feeling of low-grade nausea. Clearly, many similarities abound.

Although there are many similarities between anaphylaxis and the reactions experienced by Larry and Raja, most noteworthy is the systemic progression of seemingly unrelated symptoms that effect everything from digestion to consciousness. As a known allergic response, anaphylaxis is responsible for physical, emotional, and cognitive changes that would also effect behavior. For example, the changes noted during anaphylactic reactions include physical changes, such as nausea, emotional changes, such as severe anxiety, and cognitive changes, such as loss of consciousness. By comparing physiological and psychological changes occurring during reactions, we see the correlation between the systemic, allergic response produced by anaphylaxis and the systemic nature of reactions experienced by Larry and Raja. The correlation between symptoms common to anaphylaxis and those experienced by Larry and Raja establishes that a reaction is a systemic, allergic response. By its very nature, an allergic response is progressive; hence, a reaction is a progressive, systemic, allergic response.

However, there is one noteworthy difference between anaphylaxis and symptoms of reactions experienced by Larry and Raja: anaphylaxis is deadly if not treated in time (9). Thankfully, the reactions experienced by Larry and Raja are not fatal. While this difference initially seemed perplexing, further research indicated that the medical intervention used to prevent death from anaphylactic shock includes the administration of adrenaline (10). This information allowed me to further hypothesize that autistic individuals self-produce adrenaline during reactions, preventing anaphylactic shock while simultaneously creating measurable differences in perception and behavior. This hypothesis is outlined below by comparing the complement cascade during normal immune response to that of a theorized complement cascade during reactions in autistic individuals.

A Complement Cascade

In joint publications produced by the National Cancer Institute and the National Institute of Allergy and Infectious Diseases, the immune response is described as a 'complement cascade' (11). In a complement cascade, "...each component is activated in turn, [which] activates the next in a precise sequence of carefully regulated steps..." (12). The complement begins by identifying an invader—a foreign particle that is incompatible with the human body and does not belong—and isolating or killing the invader, so that it may be removed. Normal invaders are antigens; antigens that stimulate an allergic response are called allergens (13). When the immune system encounters an antigen, it mounts a complicated defense that allows it identify, isolate, destroy, and discard the antigen (14). When this is complete, the body returns to a stable state.

In a normal immune response, the body is busily fighting off antigens without our knowledge because we are not experiencing symptoms that notify us that the immune system has been activated. When an allergen is encountered, however, the immune response is different, triggering reactions by immune cells that cause discomfort, swelling, and pain (15).

The discomfort, swelling, and pain result from the release of chemicals stored in specific immune cells that respond to allergens. Unfortunately, allergens are not well understood, and the information describing them is sketchy, at best. However, based on the similarities between symptoms of anaphylaxis and reactions experienced by Larry and Raja, it can be strongly speculated that autistic reactions, like anaphylaxis, represent a systemic allergic response. Additionally, we can hypothesize that systemic allergies, like anaphylaxis and autistic reactions, also have a complement cascade that represent a patterned and predictable response in the immune system. To that end, I offer the following data.

Autism's Complement Cascade

In the following exercise, I compare the symptoms of reaction with potential immune responses triggered by ingesting an allergen. I have intentionally excluded definitions of medical terminology that make this process cumbersome; however, all terminology comes from the references listed in the bibliography. Anyone wishing further clarification may find those resources helpful. Because multiple symptoms are reported on Day Two and Day Three, I have also combined these symptoms and offered a complement correlation, speculating about the exit of allergens (hence, the stable state achieved) on Day Four. Finally, I have offered my theory regarding aggravated autism, which I describe as an individual who is ingesting a steady stream of allergens, and what I speculate would happen under such circumstances with the complement cascade.

Autism's Complement Cascade
1. *Dry throat:* Complement cascade begins. IgE mount defense, mast cells and basophils release histamines and heparin. Throat becomes dry and uncomfortable.
2. *Tingling:* Tingling occurs due to the B cells massively multiplying and entering the bloodstream, and/or adrenaline enters system, as brain is activated and sends stress signal to the adrenal glands at onset of allergen.
3. *Back pain in kidney region:* Swelling due to complement/IgE activation/ multiplication. Actual swelling occurring in the kidney region, but recognized in back area as tissues swell and become painful.
4. *Sinus pain:* Complement cascade. Sinuses swelling as mast cells and basophils release histamines and heparin.
5. *Can's sit still:* Complement cascade. Brain receives warning of allergens, sends stress signal to adrenal glands. Adrenaline enters the bloodstream. Adrenaline makes it hard to sit still or focus on anything.
6. *Hot:* Complement cascade. Mast cells and basophils release histamines and heparin, which cause blood vessels to become dilated and contribute warmth. Warmth could also be contributed from adrenaline/the adrenaline response.

7. *Can't sleep*: Multiple symptoms colliding, including increased adrenaline (which may impact neurotransmitters, including serotonin, melotonin, and dopamine), joint pain and achiness from mast cells and basophils releasing histamines and heparin.

8. *Joint pain in knees and elbows*: Lymphocytes produced in long bones—the femur and the humerus. Release of lymphocytes in bloodstream impact knee and elbow joints, dispersing mast cells and basophils that cause inflammation and pain.

9. *Day Two overall achiness*: Complement cascade. Lymphocytes have multiplied and been dispersed throughout the body, causing swelling, pain, and diminished function. Multiple symptom collision has interrupted sleep, and body has not had time to rest and recover.

10. *Day Three confusion/dementia*: Possible neurochemical imbalance caused by adrenaline onslaught, and/or IgE in brain causing mast cells and basophils to disperse histamine and heparin, causing swelling/interference with normal brain function.

11. *Confusion gone by Day Four*: All lymphocytes have traveled the lymph cycle, entered the thoracic duct, and exited to the bloodstream for removal.

I believe that sound and smell sensitization is heightened in autistic individuals is the result of the adrenaline onslaught, which is connected to the "fight or flight" response. The "fight or flight" response responds to danger. If one were in a dangerous situation, he may need to have heightened smell and sound sensitivity to make an accurate choice regarding self-preservation. Unfortunately, since the autistic child is not normally in danger but the chemicals in his body cause him to behave as though he were in danger, his behavior is largely incomprehensible. Additionally, the chemical changes, including adrenaline release occurring during a reaction may influence how the autistic individual perceives visual information regarding human faces.

As part of the complement cascade, the adrenaline onslaught may be responsible for the brain reconfiguring the location in which it perceives information regarding human faces. In *Newsweek* magazine's cover story *Understanding Autism*, a picture illustrated how the normal brain processes a facial image in the fusiform gyrus, but an autistic brain processes the same facial image in the inferior temporal gyrus, which is typically used to for processing inanimate objects (16). Perhaps the brain actually switches from the fusiform gyrus to the temporal gyrus at the onset of allergens, as the stress signal triggers adrenaline and the body prepares to "fight or flee". This ingenious switch would allow an individual maximum objectivity to make the best choice for self-preservation.

Finally, I believe that the complement cascade, when triggered over and over due to ingesting allergens with every meal, could exacerbate, causing the frenzied symptoms often seen in autism. For instance, when autism is viewed through the allergy paradigm, we see that foods containing allergens cause inflammation and pain. As the pain and inflammation continues without ceasing, we see strange behaviors, such as the autistic child dragging his head on the floor or crying without consolation. Accompanied by the adrenaline burst, which also continues without ceasing, we see hyperactivity pushed to the outer limits: spinning, finger and arm flapping, or jumping until one literally falls asleep. Without respite from offending allergens, autistic children exhibit bizarre behaviors, and an inability to relate to others, that markedly set them apart. As with any other allergy, the course of treatment is to simply remove the source of allergen and watch the symptoms disappear. So, too, it appears to facilitate recovery from autism.

Identifying Foods That Trigger Reactions Using Touch and Smell

In a development occurring two months after concluding the three-day healing pattern resulting from reactions, I witnessed another phenomenon that allowed me to further my theory of autism regarding its progressive quality. While touching a nut candy I made using only honey, lemon juice, and nuts, Larry received a "jolt" that prompted him to swallow the candy. After swallowing the candy, he entered a mental stupor.

Larry's jolt and subsequent mental stupor triggered the memory of Raja's inexplicable behavior at 14 months old. As you may recall, this was the incident where Raja exhibited unusual giddiness and sloppy motor control that prompted me to photograph him. Frequently, Raja responded with a strange kind of intensity to various foods, becoming manic about eating foods that triggered this strange response. *It seemed that Larry and Raja reacted to certain foods with such intensity that the foods produced an overwhelming and involuntary response to be consumed.* This response never appeared to be related to hunger.

While Larry's jolt appeared to be an isolated event, I considered it very seriously. *He had touched the candy for less than three seconds, received the jolt, then put the candy in his mouth in what appeared to be a knee-jerk response.* Moreover, the candy contained nuts, an ingredient that Larry normally avoids because they cause him to itch. Therefore, the candy triggered something in him that forced him to override his intellectual knowledge that he should avoid the candy because it contained nuts, *eating the candy anyway.* While eating the candy produced symptoms indicating that Larry was no longer experiencing a stable state, he did not experience all the symptoms of reaction and did not require three days to heal.

Fascinated by this curious scenario, two questions emerged. First, how could Larry identify a food that would trigger a reaction by touching it for three seconds? Second, assuming he could know through touch that a food would trigger a reaction, why would he then eat it? In other words, was Larry actually identifying foods that could produce a reaction through touch, and, if so, what quality did the food possess that would cause him override the knowledge that he should not eat the food (because it makes him itch) and eat it anyway? I decided to devise a blindfolded test to see what foods Larry could identify by touch that would elicit the involuntary response to eat the food he was touching. The documentation describing the testing procedure and results follows.

Testing Foods and Ingredients by Touch

I blindfolded Larry and seated him at the dining room table. We began testing all foods in the house to see which elicited a jolt when applied to Larry's fingertips. Even if a food elicited a jolt and Larry wanted to eat it, I instructed him not to, believing that ingesting a food producing a jolt might influence the test results.

At the time we tested, our home was free of foods containing casein and gluten. We tested every edible substance in the pantry, refrigerator, and cupboards, including flours, spices, nuts, and flavorings. The flours included rice flour, potato starch flour, tapioca flour, sweet rice flour, soy flour, and other baking ingredients such as xanthum gum, carob, yeast, and various types of sugar. The flavorings contained glycerin in place of alcohol. The seasonings and spices were store purchased in whole form, including salt or pepper, to eliminate the possibility of contact with gluten. Every other substance conformed to the standards of the casein-free, gluten-free diet, including fruit, vegetables, meat, rice, nuts, and pure fruit juice.

During testing, Larry was blindfolded and sat at the dining room table. I prepared the testing substances without telling him what I was preparing to avoid mental predisposition. I placed a small quantity of the substance on a plate—perhaps the equivalent of four tablespoons—giving Larry adequate chance to handle the substance on his fingertips. He touched each substance using his first three fingers and thumb. He then smelled the substance while on his fingertips. I asked him if he wanted to ingest the substance by licking his fingers. I recorded his responses on paper. After testing one substance, Larry washed and dried his hands. We used exactly the same process with every food and ingredient tested.

One of the most fascinating aspects of this process was Larry's heightened sensitivity to smells. Using his sense of smell, he could accurately detect many substances while I was preparing them in the kitchen before I brought them to the dining room table. Interestingly, any substance that Larry could identify by smell while I was preparing it in the kitchen invariably produced the desire to be ingested. Moreover, Larry reported that certain smells, such as pepper and peppermint, elicited such a strong response that his nasal cavities and head tingled. In certain instances, his whole body began tingling, which he experienced as a pleasant sensation. When he encountered a substance that produced a tingling sensation, he smelled it for a long time, reporting where the tingling was occurring. Any substance that produced tingling also elicited the jolt.

We agreed that any substance that produced a jolt or elicited tingling during touching or smelling while blindfolded was likely to trigger a reaction if ingested. Thus, if Larry touched and smelled a substance but it did not cause tingling, I asked whether he experienced the jolt and wished to ingest the substance. Any substance that Larry desired to ingest was considered very likely to trigger a reaction. Any substance Larry did not want to ingest was considered neutral. Any substance considered very likely to trigger a reaction was eliminated from the diet and removed from our home.

The Pleasant Effects Accompanying a Jolt

When I asked Larry what sensations he experienced after reacting to the jolt by eating the candy, he replied that ingesting the candy brought a sense of satisfaction. Additionally, he said that the candy gave him a "rush" and produced the pleasant sensation all over his body, like he was getting something that he needed. He could not tell me why he chose to eat the candy despite it containing nuts, which otherwise make him itch, and why he was willing to experience the annoying itching associated with the nuts for the benefit of experiencing the candy. He only said that the moment he received the jolt, he knew he needed to eat the candy, putting it in his mouth without considering the effects of the nuts. He described the sensation of the jolt as an indicator that he *had* to eat the candy. When he experienced the jolt, he had an overwhelming urge to eat the candy, knowing it would feed something inside him that wanted to feel the rush.

Larry indicated that once he ate the candy, something inside of him was satisfied. I asked him if the sensation that needed satiating was hunger. He replied that it was not a physical hunger but a different kind of hunger. He said it was like a craving, only it was so strong it consumed his attention, demanding to be satisfied. Once he ate the candy, the sensation went away, replaced by the pleasant effects produced by eating the candy.

The Source of the Jolt

After lengthy consideration, I hypothesized that the jolt Larry received by touching a piece of candy for three seconds is an indicator that his body has been trained to retain cellular knowledge of foods that will produce a "rush" upon ingestion. Furthermore, I posit that the rush associated with ingesting foods that produce a jolt is actually an adrenaline rush produced by the immune system. I also believe that said adrenaline rush is addictive for two reasons. First, the initial effects of an immune response are described as pleasant experiences (the rush and tingling sensation). Second, anticipation of the rush supersedes knowledge to the contrary not to eat a food for other reasons. Thus, the cellular training resulting in the ability to touch foods and determine whether they will produce a rush upon ingestion is a shortcut developed in relation to an addiction to adrenaline, which is a self-produced chemical naturally occurring when an allergen contacts the immune system.

As previously documented, we know that the immune response is connected with the brain and that the brain sends stress signals to the adrenal glands which pump adrenaline into the bloodstream. I believe that the jolt Larry experienced is an adrenaline response that results from the signals sent to Larry's brain the moment his fingers contacted the candy. His brain then sent a message to his adrenal glands, which pumped a burst of adrenaline in his bloodstream, resulting in the jolt. If this seems impossible, consider that I can actually witness the jolt. From a self-preservation standpoint, it seems entirely plausible that the body could encode immune response information and train parts of the body representing the first line of defense to interpret such information in a matter of seconds. Rather than the brain and fingertips being separate entities, perhaps the brain's wisdom is encapsulated in the fingertips. Instead of communicating back and forth between fingertips and brain, the brain is actually part of the fingertips as part of the immune system. Thus, a jolt can be produced within three seconds of touching a food because the brain has educated the cells in the first line of defense regarding allergens to help prevent unnecessary immune responses. Thus an allergenic food can be determined within three seconds of touching a food.

However, if it is true that the brain is constantly retraining the cellular memory in the body parts representing our first line of immune defense to ward off allergens, what would account for the reversal of judgment evident in ingesting foods that trigger an immune response?

One possibility is the heightened and pleasant sensations experienced during the Day One phase of an immune response. As previously documented, Larry describes those sensations as a pleasant "buzz" or rush. I believe that the buzz experienced during Day One is associated with adrenaline utilized by the immune system while encountering allergens. Moreover, I believe that it is the adrenaline, not the food that results in adrenaline production, which is actually addictive. What is not understood is why an individual develops an addiction to adrenaline.

The Progressive Quality of Addiction

If we can entertain the possibility that an individual becomes addicted to adrenaline, which is naturally stimulated during an immune response, we can likewise entertain the notion that the body begins to crave foods that trigger an adrenaline rush, training itself to identify such foods through touch. Like a drug addiction, there is a progressive quality to adrenaline addiction, such that the body becomes acclimated to the amount that originally triggered a rush, eventually requiring more of the same substance to elicit the expected rush. While I do not claim to know much about the dynamics of addiction, it has been through dismantling the autistic symptoms evidenced in Larry and Raja that I have postulated certain ideas about autism's progressive quality as it relates to addiction. Moreover, while I could not explain how it was that Raja *entered* his downward developmental spiral that eventually led to diagnosable autism, I can speculate with relative accuracy that he has entered recovery by *removing* foods that triggered an immune response. Thus, it is from hindsight that I theorize that autism is progressive, systemic, allergic response. It is the hindsight gained during the course of dismantling autism and watching how quickly recovery is derailed through contact with food that interrupts a stable state and produces a reaction.

As previously noted, when Larry ate the candy, he did manifest symptoms of a derailed stable state but did not experience all the symptoms associated with the three-day healing pattern. Initially, I noticed that Larry was in a mental stupor and that his eyes were dilated. Subsequent symptoms became apparent thereafter, including thick and slow speech, following rather than initiating activities, and becoming easily aggravated. His eyes were dull. He seemed listless. His reaction time, mentally and conversationally, was markedly slow, as though it was taking a long time to hear and process information. He acted like he was drunk, although without notable physical sloppiness.

Interestingly, Larry did not notice that he was manifesting symptoms of a reaction. When I asked him if he felt he was having a reaction, he did not comment but looked at me as though he did not know what I was talking about. His glazed eyes and dazed mannerisms reminded me of Raja at 14 months old. Larry did not appear able to appropriately interpret, or respond to, information or surroundings. In that moment, I hypothesized that Raja's reaction at 14 months old was a precursor of diagnosable autism resulting from progressive, systemic responses to food containing allergens. Thus, Raja's diagnosable autism did not occur overnight. It manifested in small steps beginning with subtle symptoms such as mental stupor, the inability to listen and respond appropriately, and mood swings, manifesting as diagnosable autism over time.

Just as the physical symptoms indicate a progressive, systemic response, so too the mental and emotional symptoms are systemic, changing over time. It is easy to miss the moodiness and mental stupor if not paying close attention because the symptoms subside in several hours. To my recollection, Raja manifested these symptoms only once, at 14 months old, never manifesting them again. However, it may be more accurate to say that Raja's behavior and demeanor became asymptomatic. In other words, it is quite likely that symptoms such as these manifested time and again but were absorbed by Raja's changing cognition and disposition. Over time, the loss of a stable state would make it impossible to judge when such manifestations occurred. Given my understandings regarding autism as a progressive, systemic response, I suspect this is true.

In retrospect, the mental stupor and associated symptoms are a step in autism's progressive downward spiral. At 14 months old, Raja's symptoms were an early indicator that his entire body was developing a system of identifying foods and substances that trigger a mental and emotional response initially experienced by him as pleasant. As he touched and ate foods that elicited the pleasant response associated with the adrenaline rush, he learned which of them triggered that response. Such cellular knowledge became encoded in his fingertips, giving him the ability to identify allergenic foods on contact. Eventually, the desire to elicit the pleasant "buzz" associated with certain foods led to a self-limited diet, eating only those foods that produced a buzz. When an allergenic food that produces such a buzz is contacted over and over again, it will continually produces an adrenaline rush. It is precisely this adrenaline rush that is responsible for the myriad social and behavioral manifestations associated with diagnosable autism.

Summary

The disorder that emerges as autism begins with an impulse to stimulate the pleasant adrenaline rush produced by the brain in response to foods and substances to which the body is allergic. This process becomes addictive. However, it is not the food and substances, in and of themselves, that contain addictive components. It is the allergic response, and perhaps just adrenaline itself, to which the individual becomes addicted. Addicted to adrenaline, the body actually becomes confused, desiring to contact or ingest foods and substances that cause an allergic response because it is in the allergic response that the individual receives the adrenaline rush.

Children begin self-limiting their diets in an attempt to discern which foods and substances produce an allergic response, providing an adrenaline rush they experience as pleasant. Initially, this adrenaline rush effects behavior, including emotion, cognition, and/or motor control. Over time, however, the individual becomes sensitized to the foods. As the entire cascade grows, the individual is further impaired mentally, emotionally, and physically. Slowly, the child's behavior and demeanor alter, and desire for social interaction ceases. Eventually, all the seemingly unrelated physical, mental, and emotional symptoms fit the paradigm of autism. Diagnosable autism becomes apparent.

It is quite plausible that the perplexing behaviors associated with autism are the result of an unabated onslaught of adrenaline triggered by foods producing an allergic response, such as arm flapping, head banging, or jumping until one literally falls asleep. If allergens are ingested so rapidly that the body does not have the requisite three days to recover before ingesting another round of allergens, the immune response is constantly triggered. Receiving a steady stream of adrenaline may also effect the part of the brain that perceives human faces, reversing it from that which has affect to that which is inanimate. Additionally, adrenaline is responsible for the "fight or flight" response. As part of the fight or flight response, adrenaline may be responsible for heightened sensitivity to noises, smells, and touch. It may also lead to a heightened sense of aggression or desire to be aggressive when confronted by others.

It is helpful to realize that a progressive, systemic, allergic response naturally produces a chemical reaction that causes swelling, and swelling causes pain. It is probable that all autistic children are in a constant state of pain. Moreover, it is possible that said pain makes learning and socializing difficult. Pain may also be responsible for moodiness common in autistic children, including crying, screaming, and upset when routines are violated. Pain is very difficult to cope with, especially for children. Perhaps understanding their physical predicament will elicit our swift and compassionate response to design a medically supervised recovery center for autistic children, whereby the dual goals of scientific testing and recovery are combined under one roof.

Until the theory is proven that diagnosable autism represents the cumulative effect of progressive, systemic allergic responses to food and environmental stimuli, we can facilitate recovery and developmental gain by using the techniques outlined in this text. to achieve and maintain a stable state. Additionally, we can inform parents that autism is not a hopeless disorder. The road to recovery may be bumpy, but the results are life altering and miraculous in every way. The only requirement is to err on the side of healing and embrace a plausible theory that has yet to be proven. In time, the results may literally speak for themselves!

Resources

The following resources may offer additional information on topics related to the implementation of Comprehensive Organic Intervention.

Autism Treatment Center of America
The Son-Rise Program at the Option Institute
2080 S. Undermountain Road
Sheffield, MA 01257
(413) 229-2100
E-mail: *sonrise@option.org.*

The Tahoma Clinic
Dr. Jonathan V. Wright
Author of *Dr. Wright's Guide To Healing With Nutrition*
515 West Harrison Street
Kent, WA 98032
(253) 854-4900
www.tahoma-clinic.com

Special Foods!
9207 Shotgun Court
Springfield, VA 22153
(703) 644-0991

Carol Simontacchi,
Author of *The Crazy Makers: How the Food Industry Is Destroying Our Brains and Harming Our Children*
5670 W. Cypress Street, Suite C
Tampa, FL 33607
E-mail: Csimontacchi@Vitalcast.com
www.TheCrazyMakers.com

Mothers For Natural Law
-Actively opposes genetically modified food.
-Seeking labeling of all food.
1-800-REAL-FOOD

American Academy of Allergy, Asthma and Immunology
-Comprehensive collection of journal article summaries
-Wide range of public education materials
www.aaaai.org

Center for Food Safety
www.centerforfoodsafety.org

Whole Foods Markets
www.wholefoodsmarket.com

Children's Environmental Health Program
www.checnet.org

Mothers and Others for a Livable Planet
www.mothers.org

Center for Ethics and Toxins
www.cetos.org

Peter D'Adamo, N. D.
Author of *Eat Right For Your Type*
2009 Summer Street
Stamford, CT 06905
www.dadamo.com

Melissa Diane Smith
Co-author of *Syndrome X: The Complete Nutritional Guide To Prevent And Reverse Insulin Resistance*
www.syndromeX.com

Books

Carolee Bateson-Koch, D.C., N.D.
Allergies: Disease in Disguise
Alive Books
ISBN 0-920470-42-4

Doris Sarjeant and Karen Evans
Hard to Swallow: The Truth About Food Additives
Alive Books
ISBN 0-920470-47-5

Dr. Russell L. Blaylock
Excitotoxins: The Taste That Kills
Available through *www.patlee.com*
E-mail: *info@patlee.com*

References

1. U.S. Department of Health and Human Services, *Understanding the Immune System,* NIH publication, No. 92-529, pg. 1.

2. U.S. Department of Health and Human Services, *The Immune System—How It Works*, NIH publication, No. 92-3229, pg. 15.

3. U.S. Department of Health and Human Services, *The Immune System—How It Works,* NIH publication, No. 92-3229, pg. 2.

4. U. S. Department of Health and Human Services, *The Immune System—How It Works,* NIH publication, No. 92-3229, pg. 15.

5. Bateson-Koch, Carolee, D. C., N.D., *Allergies: Disease in Disguise*, Alive Books, 1994, pg. 16.

6. Bateson-Koch, Carolee, D. C., N.D., *Allergies: Disease in Disguise*, Alive Books, 1994, pg. 16.

7. Bateson-Koch, Carolee, D. C., N.D., *Allergies: Disease in Disguise*, Alive Books, 1994, pg. 16.

8. American Academy of Allergy, Asthma and Immunology, Public Resource Center, *Tips to Remember: What is Anaphylaxis? www.aaaai.org*, 8-5-00, pg. 1.

9. American Academy of Allergy, Asthma and Immunology, Public Resource Center, *Tips to Remember: What is Anaphylaxis? www.aaaai.org*, 8-5-00, pg. 2.

10. American Academy of Allergy, Asthma and Immunology, Public Resource Center, *Tips to Remember: What is Anaphylaxis? www.aaaai.org*, 8-5-00, pg. 2.

11. National Cancer Institute and the National Institute of Allergy and Infectious Diseases, *Understanding The Immune System*, NIH Publication No. 92-529, 1991, pp. 10.

12. National Cancer Institute and the National Institute of Allergy and Infectious Diseases, *Understanding The Immune System*, NIH Publication No. 92-529, 1991, pp. 10.

13. National Cancer Institute and the National Institute of Allergy and Infectious Diseases, *The Immune System—How It Words*, NIH Publication No. 92-3229, June, 1992, pg. 2.

14. National Cancer Institute and the National Institute of Allergy and Infectious Diseases, *Understanding The Immune System*, NIH Publication No. 92-529, 1991, pg. 1-18.

15. National Cancer Institute and the National Institute of Allergy and Infectious Diseases, *Understanding The Immune System*, NIH Publication 92-529, 1991, pg. 20.

16. Newsweek Magazine, *Understanding Autism*, July 31, 2000, pg. 48.

Index

www.ingramcontent.com/pod-product-compliance
Lightning Source LLC
Chambersburg PA
CBHW061245280526
45784CB00002B/639